The Devil
We Don't
Know

The Devil We Don't Know

The Dark Side of Revolutions in the Middle East

NONIE DARWISH

WILEY

John Wiley & Sons, Inc.

Lyrics to "Trading My Sorrows" on page 83 by Darrell Evans. Copyright © 1998 Integrity's Hosanna! Music (ASCAP) (adm. at EMICMGPublishing.com) All rights reserved. Used by permission. International Copyright Secured. All Rights Reserved. Used by Permission.

Photo on page 126 from Al Azhar Mosque and University.

Published by John Wiley & Sons, Inc., Hoboken, New Jersey
Published simultaneously in Canada

For general information about our other products and services, please contact our Customer Care Department within the United States at (800) 762-2974, outside the United States at (317) 572-3993 or fax (317) 572-4002.

Wiley also publishes its books in a variety of electronic formats and by print-on-demand. Some content that appears in standard print versions of this book may not be available in other formats. For more information about Wiley products, visit us at www.wiley.com.

Library of Congress Cataloging-in-Publication Data:
Darwish, Nonie.
    The devil we don't know: the dark side of revolutions in the Middle East/Nonie Darwish. –1
    p. cm.
    Includes index.
        ISBN 978-1-118-13339-2 (cloth); ISBN 978-111-8-19789-9 (ebk);
    ISBN 978-111-8-19790-5 (ebk); ISBN 978-111-8-19791-2 (ebk)
    1. Middle East–Politics and government–21st century. 2. Revolutions–Middle East. 3. Islam and politics–Middle East. 4. Democratization–Middle East. I. Title.
    DS63.18.D37 2012
    956.05′4–dc23

                                                                    2011042288

Printed in the United States of America
10 9 8 7 6 5 4 3 2 1

To Mohammed and Mohammed, two talented young men who left Islam, but are unable to escape the hell of the Islamic state

Contents

Acknowledgments

I want to thank my three children for their smiles, love, and support. I especially want to thank my many friends in the Middle East, who kept me informed and inspired me with their courage and convictions.

I also thank my agent, Lynne Rabinoff, for her advice and professionalism.

I am very grateful to my editor Hana Lane, who brought out the best in what I wrote, and, of course, to my publisher, John Wiley and Sons, and all of the staff there for their talent and care.

Introduction

Revolutions across the Middle East are rapidly unraveling before our eyes, telling us the sad truth that Islamic uprisings eventually crawl back to where they came from—back to tyranny. If anyone has any doubt as to the negative dynamics of sharia (the religious law of Islam) and its subversive effect on society, all that person needs to do is study Islamic revolutions and why they eventually fail to achieve their goals of freedom and democracy. If you believe that sharia is a harmless religious law that Muslims have the right to practice wherever they go, I advise you to take a front seat and watch the drama unfold. The reason Islamic revolutions end in failure is because sharia forbids freedom of speech and religion, as well as gender equality and religious equality, and will remove any ruler from office if he refuses to conduct jihad and advocates peace with non-Muslim nations.

Months after the revolution in Egypt, Tahrir Square is still full of rage, anger, and divisiveness, with huge crowds that are still demanding democracy. On July 29, 2011, secularists, who are the minority, planned a sit-in called "Friday of Popular Will and Unification" when they were overwhelmed by tens of thousands of Muslim Brotherhood and Salafi groups, who called the event "Sharia Friday" and demanded an Islamic state.

Chants were heard: "Obama, Obama—we are all Osama." A large poster read "You are in our hearts and we will never forget you" and showed photos of Osama bin Laden; Hamas Shaikh Ahmad Yassin; the Libyan fighter Omar Mukhtar; the founder of the Muslim Brotherhood, Hassan al-Banna; the leader of the Brotherhood who was assassinated by President Abdel Nasser, Sayyid Qutb; and the blind man Shaikh Omar Abdel Rahman, who is being held in a U.S. prison. The square was full of Saudi flags symbolizing the Islamist state under Allah and the Islamic sword.

While most nations around the world have realized the failures of theocracy, many Muslims around the world are still carrying signs with the Muslim Brotherhood slogan "Islam is the solution." This catchy phrase appeals to the Muslim masses, who have never learned the difference between religion and the political system, and whose votes in the coming elections across the Middle East will decide what kind of political system they will live under. If the slogan carries the day, any secular democracy movement in Cairo or other Arab capitals will be left at the mercy of the pro-sharia majority.

The trend in the Muslim world is toward restoring Allah's law as a political solution, to create the perfect Islamic state that many dream of and that never actually existed. In almost all Muslim countries that have freedom movements today, the constitutions are sharia-based, making it an act of apostasy to attempt to remove sharia from the future constitutions. Not one demonstrator in the streets of Cairo carried a sign asking for the removal of sharia from the new constitution of Egypt's future government, a government that people expect to miraculously bring them freedom and democracy.

The fourteen-hundred-year history of Islam tells us that Muslims have no confidence in secular government. The banner "Islam is the solution" itself holds democracy in contempt. The questions that Arab revolutionaries today must ask themselves include: Are Muslims confident and secure enough in their faith and its survival to stop requiring the government and the legal system to enforce Islam under penalty of death? Why do Muslims not dare remove sharia from their constitutions? Why do they dread letting go of total control of every aspect of a Muslim's life and the institutions that govern him? What is behind their fears and insecurity? What forces them to rely on government and not on the freedom of the Muslim individual to choose?

The purpose of this book is not simply to criticize Islam or point out Islam's failures in order to tear it down. First and foremost, I want to explain what lies behind the revolutions in the Middle East and to expose Islam for what it is: a belief system that will inevitably doom those revolutions. Islam and its sharia cannot coexist with freedom and democracy.

This book is also a plea for Muslims to face the truth as a first step toward fulfilling the aspirations of the young Muslim demonstrators all over the Middle East who are risking their lives and shedding their blood for freedom. It is a plea to take responsibility for Islam's bloody confrontation with non-Muslims and nations around the world. Muslims who truly love their religion and who want it to survive and thrive will put aside their pride and shame, lay down their guns, and honestly acknowledge the plight and challenges of Islam today, not only for themselves, but also for the rest of the world. Redemption, asking for forgiveness, and evolving to a better self are values that apply to everyone, every religion and ideology, if they are to stand the test of time. Islam and Muslims are no exception, and the whole world will stand in support of such a movement. In fact, this has already happened; we have seen people around the world praying for the success of the oppressed Muslim demonstrators across the Middle East. I, for one, wept with pride for my people and my culture of origin. Muslims who are willing to stand up and admit their imperfections to themselves and the world have nothing to fear. That is the most positive, constructive, and honorable thing Muslims can do today.

This book will not determine whether Islam can be reformed; only Muslims themselves can make that choice. Yet I will lay out the challenge that Muslims must take up to bring into being a much-needed reformation movement. Based on the truth, this movement must reject old patterns of behavior, such as denial, making excuses, finger-pointing, and a deep fear of being exposed to shame. Without welcoming the truth, any reformation of Islam will be doomed to failure. For Muslims to continue with the status quo will waste the heroic efforts of young Muslims who shed their blood in Tahrir Square and other countries in the Middle East. Insisting, as the Islamists do, that Islam's enormous problems are simply due to misinterpretation and misunderstanding will not save Muslims and the rest of the world from future bloody confrontations. This juvenile attitude will only exasperate Muslims and non-Muslims alike.

Most people, myself included, don't want to criticize any religion, let alone the religion they were born into. Religion must be, first and foremost, a personal relationship with God. Yet if people acting in the name of religion expand its sphere of control until their country becomes a one-party totalitarian state, then these coreligionists have overstepped their bounds. If this state preserves an elaborate legal system that can put someone to death for disagreeing with sharia, then it is trampling on the human rights of its citizens. If this state has a military mandate called jihad that violates the sovereignty of non-Muslim countries, then Islam is no longer a private matter, immune from criticism. Islam placed itself in the realm of criticism the day it demanded to become a political system with imperialist aspirations. If an ideology, religious or secular, has assumed for itself such totalitarian rights over others, then others have the right to challenge, discredit, and defeat it.

Islam is challenging the world but has made it a crime for others to challenge it. This book will challenge Islam, not for the purpose of shaming Muslims, but to expose the truth and encourage reformation. Having seen for ourselves what Islam has done to the lives and the political systems of Muslim countries, we who live in free democracies have a duty to criticize and scrutinize Islam. If our criticism inspires Muslims to reform, then it will have achieved an honorable goal.

As it is practiced today, Islam is the problem, not the solution.

1

The Cycle
of Dictatorships
and Revolutions

When I look back on my university days in Tahrir (Liberty) Square in the center of downtown Cairo, I remember a space and a time very different from the revolutionary scene that mesmerized the world on January 25, 2011. As a student, I often walked along the dusty and poorly paved sidewalks that led to the American University in Cairo, which is located on one of its corners. All around me were thousands of Egyptians, arriving from the surrounding suburbs and going in different directions. They bumped into one another and rarely apologized, because there was no way to avoid getting in the way of other people. The pedestrian was, and still is, responsible for jumping out of the way of cars. Even in the center of Cairo, roads are not designed for traffic. Traffic signals are scarce, and, where they do exist, they are ignored.

The traffic situation was bad then and is much worse now that the population of Egypt has more than doubled. In my student days, I could not avoid being rubbed against, bumped into, and even groped or pinched by sexually frustrated men who seemed to seize every opportunity for physical contact whenever a woman was alone without a man. It was a constant reminder of a women's place in the Islamic state: the home.

Those were the oppressive days of another dictator, Gamal Abdel Nasser. Unlike 2011, in the late 1960s people did not demonstrate to get rid of a dictator, but rather to keep him in power. After Egypt's humiliating defeat by Israel in the 1967 war, when Nasser resigned from office, Egyptians took to the streets to bring him back, fearful of letting go of their "daddy" dictator, even if he might lead them off a cliff to defeat and tyranny. The Egyptian people have come a long way since then.

Tahrir Square today has become a landmark of Egypt's January 25th revolution, which ousted the thirty-year rule of Hosni Mubarak. The world was on edge as it watched the developments of the Middle East uprisings with empathy and hope for a people yearning for freedom. The images on TV were riveting, inspirational, and a reminder to everyone of the power of the human spirit when confronted with repression. I saw a new generation of young Egyptians with V-signs who painted their faces with the color of the Egyptian flag, much as Westerners often do at sports events. The appeal of Western popular culture remains strong in the Middle East, despite the constant anti-Western propaganda. Having lived for thirty years in Egypt, I could almost read the minds of those people, starving for freedom and dignity in the Cairo streets. They wanted to reach out to the West and cry, "Help us, we want freedoms like yours!" Many protesters were eager to speak to Western journalists and carried posters with sayings in English such as "Game Over" specifically to communicate with the West.

With youthful passion, protesters charged into the streets, telling their loved ones, "I won't come back." They were ready to die in that square to end centuries of oppression and achieve the freedom that most people in the West take for granted. My heart went out to my countrymen as I watched them risk their lives to confront guns and tanks of their own military and police, aimed against them. A feeling of pride dominated my mixed emotions when I saw Egyptians finally say no to a chronic state of enslavement under oppressive dictatorships and police states. Then the unique spirit of the Egyptian people truly blossomed when the military chose to stand by the people and guard the welfare of the nation.

Even though Mubarak was a dictator and had a hard time letting go, to his credit he had the decency not to use the full power of his military and police, as other dictators in Iran, Libya, and Syria have done against protesters in the streets. Mubarak also refused to leave Egypt, subjecting himself to be tried or executed. The Mubarak family has been put under house arrest, and Mubarak and his two sons are in jail, awaiting trial and facing execution if they are found guilty. It is a tragedy on all levels and is the ugly side of revolutions.

All of the various factions, Islamists, socialists, intellectuals, Christians, and ordinary Arabs on the street had one
thing in common: they all wanted to oust the dictator. Even
though the revolution seemed spontaneous, every group,
especially Islamists, has talked about the removal of all Arab
dictators for several decades. Calls to depose Mubarak and
others were openly expressed at many Muslim events in
the West. To the Islamist, Muslim leaders in power were
not Muslim enough, because they obstructed the Islamists'
demands for a pure Islamic state. Young reformists and certain intellectuals with a passion for Western-style democracy thought their leaders were not democratic enough.
Christians believed they were discriminated against and that
Mubarak did nothing to protect them. As for the ordinary
man on the street, he was simply fed up with thirty years of
dictatorship.

The West, in large part, has misunderstood what happened and why. The crux of the misunderstanding has been
a description of the regimes of Hosni Mubarak, Bashar
al-Assad, Sadam Hussein, and others as secular, when in
reality they were not. Many of these dictators did come from
a military background, and their wives did not wear Islamic
clothes. Yet some, in their youth, had been members of the
Muslim Brotherhood—for example, Gamal Abdel Nasser
and Anwar El Sadat. No Muslim leader in the Middle East
can get away with truly secular rule or even survive one day
in office if he rejects Islamic law. It was during Mubarak's
rule in 1991 that Egypt signed the Cairo Declaration for
Human Rights, which declared that sharia, the divine law
of Islam, supersedes any other law. So, even though sharia
is not applied 100 percent in Egypt, Syria, Iraq, Jordan, or

Tunisia, it is officially the law of the land. Mubarak, like all Muslim leaders, had to appease the Islamists to avoid their wrath. In fact, according to sharia, a Muslim head of state has to rule by Islamic law and preserve Islam in its original form or he must be removed from office. Islamic law leaves no choice for any Muslim leader but to accept, at least officially, that sharia is the law of the land. Otherwise, he will be ousted by the mob, which is commanded by sharia to remove any leader who is not a Muslim. Because of that law, Muslim leaders must play a game of appearing Islamic and anti-West, while trying to get along with the rest of the world. It's a game with life-or-death consequences.

The tension between what Islam really demands of Muslims and trying to get along with the West has always been a problem that Muslim leaders must deal with, whether they are in Pakistan, Saudi Arabia, Egypt, Jordan, or elsewhere in the Middle East. This tension has been building for a long time, lurking on the horizon, and it finally exploded. Although the revolt was inspired by events in Tunisia, it had strong roots in Muslim society and customs. The spark that caused the downfall of the twenty-three-year-old dictatorship of the Tunisian leader Zine el Abidine Ben Ali was an incident of gross injustice to the common man. A policewoman slapped a twenty-six-year-old street vendor and confiscated his goods for a permit violation. Note that when a woman in the Muslim world is given the chance to have a man's job, the oppression that she feels in that world often causes her to oppress those weaker and poorer than herself. It is the opposite of what we see in Western movies, when a woman slaps a man and his reaction is not humiliation but a smile. In the

Muslim world, a man would feel the utmost humiliation after being slapped on the face by a woman. In Tunisia, the policewoman's uniform was her only protection against being slapped back. The street vendor was not only humiliated in public, but his livelihood was also taken away, in a country that suffers from extreme poverty and a high rate of unemployment. Out of desperation, he set himself on fire in public and died. Many of his countrymen identified with him, and a revolt spontaneously erupted. The street vendor became a martyred symbol of the revolution.

The tragedy struck a chord across the Muslim world with those who identified with the poor man's humiliation, hopelessness, and despair. In Islamic chat rooms, people called the policewoman's behavior "un-Islamic" and explained that this is not how Muslims should behave toward one another. The word *un-Islamic* has become a common expression used by Muslims who want to separate themselves from the misbehavior of other Muslims. They use the word as a way to defend Islam and to deny that this religion is responsible for what Muslim society has produced. That stance ignores the reality of how a totalitarian religion such as Islam influences the entirety of how a society functions with its good, bad, and ugly sides. The Islamic system has clearly failed to channel the problem of human aggression and oppression toward one's fellow man and instead has perpetuated it. It has failed to promote love and respect for mankind as a whole as the basic principle from which all love and respect emanate. Islamic commandments clearly restrict compassion and friendship only to fellow Muslims and advocate mistreatment, hatred, and violence to non-Muslims. This distinction between how to treat Muslims and all others does not bring out the best in the human character and leaves Muslims in a state of confusion in their interpersonal relationships.

Being a citizen of a Muslim country is a challenge to one's ability to maintain a healthy lifestyle. I remember watching horrific scenes of police brutality on the streets of Cairo, where poor people and those with menial jobs were slapped and humiliated by not only the police but any person of authority and power. This is still true today. Anyone who had money to bribe the authorities could literally get away with murder. Others, and they are the majority, had to endure a grinding life of constant abuse and oppression from the top down. The oppression could not have become so prevalent in the political system and the police without having first infecting all levels of Muslim society. Maids are often still treated as slaves; slavery has always been an important Arab institution, which was never abolished by Islam and was legally practiced in Saudi Arabia until 1962.

While mosques are busy teaching Muslims how to hate Jews and mistreat Christians, they make no time to preach to them about forgiveness, redemption, and how to treat one another and to value individual rights and human dignity. What makes the problem even worse is that Muslims are told by sharia that they have the right to force its law on others. Muslims are told that they will not be prosecuted for killing an apostate or an adulterer, and that their law gives the Muslim individual, in many cases, the right to be judge and executioner. Such religious laws encourage the creation of little dictators in all ranks of society, from top to bottom.

Life in Muslim society is oppressive on every level. Men are forced to perform violent jihad, and the oppression of women, gender segregation and taboos, the criminalization of free speech, and polygamy are almost universally practiced. Not all of this is the fault of the government or the police, but every type of oppression arises from the basic laws of Islam. Yet the majority of Muslims do not see the link between their oppression and sharia, which Muslims are entrusted with enforcing. Abuse and hostility can erupt from anyone in a position of power: bosses over workers, husbands over wives. Child abuse is at an epidemic level, and even neighbors feel entitled to spy on other neighbors. Gossip is rampant and has a huge impact in a shame-based culture.

The Islamic state is the direct cause of such social ills, which, when compounded, can cause unbearable pressure on the psyches of Muslim citizens. Left with no coping mechanisms—dealing with shame without punitive consequences, freedom to speak one's mind and respect for individual dignity and privacy—the Muslim turns to warped measures to avoid detection. When distrust and anger prevail in a society, democracy and freedom will necessarily suffocate, only to be replaced with tyranny. Even if it is tyranny with the best intentions, it sets in motion a cycle of boiling rage, similar to a pressure cooker in which steam must be released periodically through violence and revolutions. One simple lesson in human behavior—respect for all mankind—that free societies learned from the outset to minimize instability was never learned in ancient civilizations such as Persia and Egypt. Unfortunately, Islam has not enabled Muslim society to escape the fate of rogue states and banana republics.

The Islamic state has one mechanism it uses to release the built-up pressure caused by the tyranny of Islamic law: it channels the people's rage and frustration to explode outside of the system in a continuous confrontation with the non-Muslim world. In this dynamic, villains must be found outside the system: Israel, the United States, past injustices, colonialism, or the Crusades are or have been good excuses for Islamic violence. The outside world has become the great Satan that is always conspiring against Muslims to cause a fitna, which means "disbelief and chaos." For instance, the threat that Osama bin Laden posed to the Saudi kingdom was channeled toward the West with the blessings and all of the financial and moral support of the Muslim world. The end result is that a majority of the people are confused, their trust and moral standards are shattered, and their concept of reality distorted.

When I was a citizen of the Muslim world, I never connected the dots between the duty of jihad; the lack of freedom; the hatred of non-Muslims, especially Jews; the totalitarian control of the Islamic state; and the sacred cows that all Muslims must worship. This colossal scheme whitewashes the requirements of sharia and protects the totalitarian system, while at the same time providing an outlet to dump blame and built-up anger outside the system. It's a plan brilliantly designed to let Muslims have their cake and eat it, too, but how long can this warped situation continue? So far, it has succeeded for fourteen hundred years without collapsing and has its roots in the harsh tribal Arabian Peninsula culture.

The propaganda, the lies, and blaming the outside world can go only so far. Sooner or later, Muslims will revolt against the symbol of their system, the head of the state. This pattern has continued for generations. No one asks why Muslims have a chronic system of dictatorship or investigates other factors in their religion or culture that contribute to the dysfunctional vicious circle of tyrannies and revolutions. The Muslim mind has been trained for centuries to look outside for reasons for Islamic failures. No one can dare publicly blame oppression on sharia, because doing that is considered an act of apostasy punishable by death. That is true tyranny, the religious tyranny of sharia, when the public is not even aware of or allowed to consider who its true oppressor is.

During the Arab Spring, not one person among the more than 10 million citizens of Tunisia, the 80 million Egyptians, or the more than 350 million citizens of all Arab countries combined had the guts to carry a sign that dared to look beyond the dictator. No one dared to openly demand the removal of sharia as the basis of law for Islamic governments. Whether it was the Egyptian revolution of 1919, 1952, or 2011, the change demanded has only been cosmetic and has always been about removal of the leader or the British. Somehow, the Muslim mind freezes whenever it considers the underlying religious ideology that is the foundation on which its systems are erected. As I watched the TV coverage of the massive protests, I was desperately searching for a brave poster proclaiming something new and daring—a poster that demanded reformation of the system and not merely removal of the dictator, along with slogans of freedom and democracy—but I could not find any. This is what I wanted to see: "Separation of mosque and state," "Removal of sharia from the Egyptian constitution," "Equal rights for all," or "Equal rights for women"—better yet, "The beating of women is not a husband's right." To my disappointment, I did not see any signs like this. As a result, I was not optimistic about how the revolution would turn out.

The anger manifested in the Arab Spring, as the uprisings were dubbed, has been bubbling for a long time. The game of blaming the West and Israel could no longer put a lid on the steam rising from the Arab street. Sadly, however, that still did not stop some in the media and the government, who live in constant denial, from accusing Israel of conspiracy and espionage and of causing the uprisings. Yet promoting jihad against the West and terrorism all over the world, especially in Israel during the last decades, was not enough for people to release their building tensions. What Arab leaders have dreaded the most was not the presumed threat of Israel, but what has erupted within their countries. Their efforts to redirect the people's anger toward Western "Satans" could no longer work. Like wildfire, the flames of the Tunisian uprising spread eastward and westward to Egypt, Yemen, Bahrain, and Syria. It produced a civil war in Libya and major protests in Morocco, Algeria, Oman, Iraq, Jordan, Saudi Arabia, the Sudan, and some of the Gulf States.

So far, the main hot spots of the revolt that succeeded in removing their dictators are Tunisia, Egypt, and Libya. In the case of the first two instances, the dictators were not Islamists and refused to make the West their enemy, as a good Muslim leader should in the eyes of the Islamists. Less tyrannical Muslim dictators who do not support the jihadists were the easier targets to take out. That explains why Zine el Abidine Ben Ali and Hosni Mubarak were ousted much more easily than Gaddafi was in Libya, plus Al Assad of Syria and Ahmedinejad of Iran are still in power. Shock waves progressively rocked Muslim governments, which rushed to suggest new reforms or promised to step down at the end of their current terms. Sudanese president Omar al-Bashir announced that he would not seek reelection in 2015; Iraq's prime minister Nouri al-Maliki, after violent demonstrations demanding his immediate resignation, also announced that he will leave office at the end of his term in 2014. Even King Abdullah of Jordan, in the face of protests, promised reforms, dissolved his cabinet, and appointed a new prime minister to form a new government. Another leader, President Ali Abdullah Saleh of Yemen, announced that he would step down within thirty days in exchange for immunity, but that has not yet happened.

As I mentioned earlier, such quick changes in government are not a new phenomenon in the Middle East. Revolutions, counterrevolutions, assassinations, and coups d'etat are commonplace in the Islamic political system. Many Muslim leaders have come to power after forceful takeovers, and, surprisingly, that is not illegal under Islamic law. Actually, it is perfectly legitimate, and when it succeeds, the masses are often jubilant and satisfied with the change. No one ever publicly accuses such new governments of illegitimacy, not even the media. An important factor in the acceptance of tyrants who take power by force is that under Islamic law, seizure of power is a legitimate way to become the ruler of a country. Sharia states, "A Calipha [Muslim head of state] is allowed to hold office through seizure of power, meaning through force" (o25.4, p. 644). I have no doubt that not one of the protesters across the Middle East ever connected this law with the political chaos of the Middle East. I have never read a single article by an Arab intellectual linking sharia to the lack of stable democracies across the Muslim world.

Amazingly, the general reaction to the Arab Spring among most Arab intellectuals was one of euphoria and high hopes. Most did not recognize the similarities to prior Islamic revolutions. Many of these began with unrealistic expectations and a denial or a fear of mentioning the true reasons for the failure of the Islamic political system. Every revolution has started with a belief that this will be the true one and that the people have finally found the formula for success. Very often in a revolution, the name of the country and its flag, its constitution, and its national anthem are changed and even history books rewritten. The narrative is always about the evil regime the revolution has overthrown and not about the religious, political, and cultural foundations of the country.

That is exactly what happened in the 1952 Egyptian revolution, but no live coverage existed to record every aspect of it, as there is today. Nasser, who headed that revolution, actually renamed the largest center of downtown Cairo "Tahrir Square," which means "Freedom Square," to signify what he claimed were the most important principles of his new revolution—freedom, democracy, and prosperity for all Egyptians. Previously, it had been called "Ismaelia Square," named after the nineteenth-century ruler Khedive Ismael, who presided over the opening of the Suez Canal. Nasser also quickly moved to change the name of Egypt to the United Arab Republic, to show that he viewed it more important to be linked to the Arab world than to Egypt's ancient history. In fact, the word *Egypt* was originally the name of the Coptic Christians of Egypt, but sometime after the Arab invasion and the Islamization of Egypt, its name was changed to "Misr," which was what the Koran called it. The West retained the traditional biblical name of Egypt until today, but Egyptians have rejected it for Islamic reasons.

In addition, Nasser changed the constitution, the national anthems, and the history books, which were rewritten to focus on the bright future of the revolution and the dark evil past of King Farouk, whom Nasser called a traitor and a puppet of the West. Nasser also changed the flag of Egypt from green with a crescent and stars to three big stripes, black signifying the dark past, white the revolution, and red the bright future. The whole Arab world adored and was inspired by the new charismatic leader; the media, artists, and singers glamorized him, and songs expressing the devotion and adoration of Nasser were heard everywhere.

Yet Nasser's revolution did not bring what Egyptians had hoped for. President Anwar Sadat, who succeeded him, made some reforms and changed the name of Egypt to include the word *Egypt* or *Misr* in Arabic. It is now the Arab Republic of Egypt. In actuality, Nasser's revolution brought one of the darkest periods of Egyptian history, with wars of aggression, poverty, tyranny, a police state, and military rule from 1952 until 2011. Since 1952, Egypt has been ruled by only three men: Nasser, Sadat, and Mubarak.

Despite Nasser's failures, however, the Egyptian revolution inspired other uprisings in the region, including the 1969 Libyan coup under Moammar Gaddafi, which ousted what he and his supporters termed the reactionary regime of King Idris. Gaddafi renamed the country, changing it from the United Kingdom of Libya to the Libyan Arab Republic. The Libyan flag was redesigned to be similar to that of Egypt's. The revolution promised to its "free brothers" a new age of prosperity, equality, and honor. In 1977,

Gaddafi, extremely fearful of coups against him, promised reforms and yet again renamed his country, this time the Great Socialist People's Libyan Arab Jamahiriya.

We can even go further back in time for other examples of the cycle of revolts against tyranny. We all remember the movie *Lawrence of Arabia*, which portrays T. E. Lawrence's support for an Arab revolt against Turkish rule in the Hijaz and a demand for autonomy from the weakened Ottoman Empire. That paved the way for a movement away from Pan-Islamism, symbolized in the Ottoman Empire, and toward Pan-Arabism, which took off later in the mid-twentieth century and eventually produced the 1952 Egyptian revolution. That revolt inspired Arabs' pride in their culture and ousted King Farouk, whose family went back in history to the Ottoman Turks and the Albanian Muslims. Yet before the overthrow of Farouk, shortly after the Arab Revolt led by Lawrence, Egypt in 1919 rebelled against the British and to establish an identity separate from the Ottoman Turks.

With the weakening of the Ottomans, Turkey officially ended the Islamic caliphate in 1922, which had held sway since 1517. The last sultan, Mehmet, was exiled, and Kemal Ataturk became the first president of the Turkish Republic. Ataturk moved quickly to turn Turkey into a secular state with a European cultural identity, rather than an Islamic or Arab identity, and even changed the Turkish alphabet to Latin, rejecting the Arabic alphabet of the Koran. The loss of the Islamic caliphate and the Turks' abandonment of their strong Islamic ties to the Arab world created a power vacuum in the Middle East. That was probably a strong factor behind Arab eagerness to find a new identity in Pan-Arabism. The loss of an Islamic unifying identity, however symbolic, was also a factor in the establishment of the Muslim Brotherhood in 1928 in Egypt.

Until recently, Turkey had isolated itself from Arab issues, especially the conflict with Israel. Yet even Turkey has not been able to escape the sweeping Islamism movement in the region and elected its first devout Muslim president in modern-day Turkey, Abdullah Gul. Under his administration, in 2010, Gul allowed the "flotilla" ships to sail out of Turkey heading to Gaza, in an act of intimidation against Israel that was very unusual for a country such as Turkey to engage in. Clearly, Turkey is now moving back to its Islamic roots.

None of the revolutions and the movements I have described accomplished their intended mission, except for Turkey, which is now moving in the direction of Islamism. Most often, Arab revolutions brought more tyranny and stagnation. A prominent example is the 1979 Islamic Iranian revolution that took out the pro-Western shah and replaced him with the most tyrannical and dangerous regime in the Middle East today. This shows that citizens of great civilizations such as Egypt, Iraq, Syria, Turkey, and Persia don't learn the lessons of their long history. With the Arab conquest that dramatically changed not only their religion, but also their language and culture, the great ancient civilizations of the region have been crippled by the impact of Islam, stumbling and falling between dictatorships and revolutions for many centuries, and there is little hope in sight. The lesson here is that the passage of time does not necessarily mean positive progress, improvement, or better results. Old civilizations are not like fine wine; they do not get better with time.

The pattern continues today. It did not take long after Mubarak stepped down for us to see the new tyranny evolving. I have many contacts in Egypt who report to me on a regular basis. I was told that the atmosphere began to get scary after religious hardliners threatened a bloodbath if anyone attempted to remove Article 2 of the Egyptian constitution, the article that states that sharia supercedes any other law, including international human rights laws. Even Mohamed El Baradei, known internationally as the director of the International Atomic Energy and who is liked by the Muslim Brotherhood, was threatened and rocks were thrown at him on the streets of Cairo when he hinted at removing Article 2. In another indication, the new military leadership issued a new law against any kissing scenes shown in movies or on TV. Feminists were being threatened and attacked.

As to the slogans proclaiming that Muslims and Christians were united in the revolution, all of that quickly evaporated. On April 14, a Christian, Major General Emad Mikhail, was appointed governor of Qena, a district that has a large Christian population. Yet the prime minister suspended the appointment after huge and violent demonstrations erupted against the appointment of a Christian to a leadership office over Muslims. Incidentally, sharia supports these Muslim rioters, which states that a Christian will not rule in an Islamic state, even over a majority Christian population. The protesters demanded a "Muslim governor in a Muslim country," chanting, "Mikhail is an infidel pig," "There is no god but Allah and Christians are the enemies of Allah," "Muslim, Muslim, will govern us" and "We will never be ruled by a Christian governor."

On April 18, after the death of two Muslims in the violence against Christians, more fighting broke out in the small southern Egyptian town of Minya, about two hundred miles south of Cairo. One Christian Copt was killed, an old woman was thrown off of her second-floor balcony, and ten Copts were hospitalized. Coptic homes, shops, businesses, fields, and livestock were plundered and torched.

In a separate horrific incident, also in April, in the southern town of Qena, about 350 miles south of Cairo, Salafis (Islamic fundamentalists) implemented an Islamic penalty, or *hudoud*, on a Christian Copt by cutting off his ear for allegedly renting his flat to a Muslim prostitute. A Muslim man who was accused of stealing motorized bicycles had his hands cut off by the hardliner Salafis, who want to follow sharia. They are no longer relying on the police to implement the justice system and are taking matters into their own hands. In this instance, they arrested the victim, judged him, and applied what they considered to be the appropriate punishment. After that, they called the police to take away the victim, saying, "We have applied the law of Allah; now come and apply your law." That sent shock waves throughout Egypt.

Attacks on Christians accelerated, and on May 7, 2011, Christian Copts were again attacked by Muslim Salafis in the area of Embaba, a suburb of Cairo. The attacks lasted for fourteen hours. The Muslims fired guns and rifles and hurled Molotov cocktails at Coptic churches, houses, and businesses. Twelve Copts were killed and 232 injured. Saint Mina Church was the first one attacked and was set on fire by some 3,000 Salafi Muslim men, because a Christian girl named Abir, who had converted to Islam after marrying a

Salafi, wanted to revert back to Christianity and was hiding inside the church.

When some Muslims objected to what the Salafis were doing, their leader publicly stated that whoever did not like Allah's law was welcome to leave the country. There were many other attacks against Christian churches, with Salafis demanding the release of another woman named Kamilya whom Muslims claimed had converted to Islam and was being held against her will at the church. The woman, the wife of a Coptic priest and a mother, appeared publicly and stated that she wanted to remain with her husband and that she was not a Muslim, but the rioters still demanded her divorce from her husband and that she be taken out of the church. Islamic rage over the Kamilya story enraged Muslims all over the Arab world and reached Islamists in Iraq, who attacked a church killing more than fifty-nine Christians, using the excuse that Christians are holding Camilia against her will. It might sound strange to people in the West, but third-party divorces are allowed in Islam. When one member of a married Christian couple converts to Islam, the two spouses are automatically divorced against their will.

The situation after the Arab Spring is clearly ushering in a new return to Islamism. The death of Osama bin Laden was mourned by the majority of Egyptians. A friend from Cairo who had secretly left Islam called me to congratulate me on the death of Osama bin Laden. He said that the majority of Egyptians were sad over the death of bin Laden and that some didn't care, but he could not find one person who was happy over the killing of the terrorist who had caused the deaths of thousands in the name of Islam. That tells us a lot about where things are heading and where the hearts of the majority of Muslims are. I am not surprised, but the West needs to understand this mind-set.

The revolutions in Egypt, Tunisia, Libya, and perhaps more to follow have succeeded in removing three dictators, but will they bring about the freedom they aspired to? Already, the future of the freedom that students and some intellectuals wanted is uncertain. Will it be an Islamic theocracy run by the extremist Salafis or a bloodbath, as they are promising?

Hearing the depressing news from Egypt, I understand why my friends have written to me that they are scared. The bearded men are all over the streets, silencing anyone who disagrees with radical Islamic law, and the majority of the illiterate and undereducated Egyptian population is following them like sheep. I am afraid for my culture of origin. I think it is going to get worse before it will ever get better.

Now, let us examine more closely in the next chapter why Islamic revolutions are doomed to fail.

2

Why Islamic
Revolutions Are
Doomed to Fail

The Arab Spring has turned out to be a fraud. A new phase of stronger tyranny has replaced the old tyranny. Have the hopeful young protesters of Tahrir Square, Tunisia, and other Middle Eastern countries been duped? How could such smart young men and women and even intellectuals and journalists not have predicted that the vacuum in power after their leaders left the stage would usher in Islamists, who represent the majority of the population?

Given the developments that unfolded so quickly after the "revolution," it is hard to grasp the initial euphoria and unrealistic optimism of the Arab Spring. Some still believe it will bring them freedom and democracy, but many of them are gradually realizing that Egypt's problems are far more complex than taking out a dictator. They voice regret that their flowery revolution has been hijacked. Whenever things do not go well, Muslims, educated or not, say it is because their best intentions were hijacked. Osama bin Ladin was adored by many in the Muslim world, who after his death hailed him as a martyr and the closest thing to a prophet. Yet Muslims in the United States would rather blame him for having hijacked Islam than engage in honest self-criticism of their religion and its jihad doctrine after 9/11. They will use any excuse, rather than go where no one can go, which is to blame Islamic teachings, jihad, and sharia for atrocities done in the name of Islam by Muslims.

As harsh as this may sound, let us look more closely at what has followed the euphoria of spring 2011. Amina Tharwat Abaza, an Egyptian media personality and the daughter of the distinguished writer and novelist Tharwat Abaza, described the deteriorating situation in postrevolutionary Egypt:

> I cannot tolerate this [coverage of church burning] any more. I had to shut off the TV, and I resigned from my position at the Egyptian TV station. I cannot be part of the crimes committed by our TV in destroying the Egyptian mind, especially among the illiterate and uneducated who are about three-quarters of our population, by befriending the murderers [the terrorists] and rejecting the open-minded.
>
> What they [Islamists] are doing is damaging Islam's reputation all over the world. This is a civil war that might evolve into a world war. The West might eventually need to occupy us to defend the

minorities. What the Salafis, extremists, the hooli-
gans are doing in Egypt is an invitation to a civil
war and a bloodbath, both internally and externally.
They are not just attacking churches, but they are
also attacking Muslim women in the streets and in
their homes. To them, Islam is condensed to a bomb,
Camilia [the Christian woman whom Muslims want
to take away from her husband because they believe
she converted to Islam], and violating churches. They
have made the whole world hate Islam but com-
plain about Islamophobia, which is the natural end
result of what you do. They created Islamophobia.
Then we make Bin Laden a heroic martyr! Are we
insane? What happened to the Egypian people? It
was once the oldest, greatest civilization on earth.
What messed up the Egyptian mind?

What is happening is unbelievable and is
depressing. If they think that these thugs can scare
us, we are not scared. They are forcing the intellectuals to go down to their level and carry weapons,
and if we must, we will. If two, three, or ten die,
then no problem. Talking to them is not working
any more. It is beyond negotiation with them. The
military council must do something. Criminals must
go to jail; those who burn and kill must go to jail.
Our military that triumphed in 1973 over Israel and
America is frozen before these thugs. The military
council says we are letting them dig their own grave
without doing anything! What kind of policy is that?
Does that mean that to prove that my neighbor is
violating me, I should allow him to kill my son? I

marched in Tahrir Square for two days, and now I
feel I was wrong, perhaps our citizens do not deserve
democracy or freedom. They deserve an enlightened
dictator, one that respects the respectable citizens
and suppresses those who abuse the system.

When she was asked where Egypt is going, Amina replied,

Egypt is already gone. Everyone I know is planning
on leaving the country, not just Christians, but also
Muslims. Terrorism is not just hurting the Christians
but it is hurting everyone. At least fifteen families I
know are getting ready to leave Egypt. They have
destroyed Egypt and we will regret the previous
administration. Getting stolen is better than getting
killed. This is not a fight over equal playing fields,
intellectuals cannot fight with bombs and knives,
they will just leave. I call on the military council to
"save your country."[1]

After President Mubarak resigned in Egypt, the Muslim
Brotherhood, which had been banned by the Mubarak
administration, has emerged more powerful and embold-
ened than ever. It has allied itself with the Salafi ultra-radical
sect to form an even more powerful Islamist presence and
moved quickly to set the agenda for the country's political future. Islamism has penetrated every institution in the
country. It became clear that anyone who wants to succeed
politically must get the blessing or approval of the Muslim
Brotherhood. Meetings occurred regularly between the
interim military government and the Brotherhood. Rumors

are starting to spread that the Muslim Brotherhood will leave the position of president to someone who is not on its membership list, on the condition that the Brotherhood will take control of the Parliament. The Brotherhood immediately made it clear that if anyone attempted to remove Article 2 of the Egyptian constitution, the article that makes sharia the law of the land, there would be a bloodbath.

As I described in chapter 1, violence against Christians, their institutions, and their homes has sharply escalated since the revolution. In early May 2011, two churches were set on fire, after Islamists attacked members of the congregation, and at least twelve people were killed and two hundred injured. There has been a systematic attempt to wipe out the Coptic Christian population, which makes up 10 percent of the nation. The situation is quickly becoming similar to the fate of Christians in the Sudan. The northern Islamic part of Sudan has systematically persecuted, enslaved, and terrorized the southern Christian part, and that fact is totally ignored by Muslims around the world. Such attacks on Christians in the area are heavily funded and supported by oil-rich Arab countries. It is rumored that thugs are often hired by the Islamists in order to place the blame on others if the conspiracy is exposed to the outside world. The armies and the Egyptian police, as well as those of all Muslim countries, are a reflection of the Islamist elements in the population, and these security forces have a huge number of Islamists in their ranks. Thus, the police and the army often stand by without doing very much while unarmed Christians are massacred. Yet they are quick to arrest injured Copts while they are being treated for their wounds.

Even when people demonstrated against the killing of Christians and the burning of their churches, the demonstrators were brazenly attacked by Muslims. Copts then protested outside the U.S. embassy in Cairo to ask for protection. This was unprecedented, because Copts have always been reluctant to ask for help from the West, for fear of being accused of allying themselves with Egypt's enemies. Yet at that point, they had no choice. The fate of the Copts looks more and more grim.

The escalating violence against the Christians reminds me of what happened in the fifties and the sixties when Egypt embarked on a campaign to purge its Jewish population. The expulsion of the Jews began after the 1952 revolution, but the purging did not end with the Jews. The hostility expanded to other minorities in Egypt, including Greeks, Italians, and Armenians, who felt that there was no place for them any longer and started to leave. Even the Muslim king Farouk, who had Ottoman roots, was criticized as not being a true Egyptian.

"First comes Saturday; then comes Sunday!" is an Islamic saying that means "First we kill the Jews, then we kill the Christians." History seems to be repeating itself in the 2011 revolution, which has begun to purge the Sunday people, the Christians. Since the time of Mohammed, it has been an Islamic mission to rid Muslim lands of Christians and Jews. Caliph Umar decreed that Jews and Christians should be removed from Arabia to fulfill a commandment the prophet gave on his deathbed: "Let there not be two religions in Arabia." That same goal became the mission of Osama bin Laden when in 1998 he issued a "Declaration of the World Islamic Front for Jihad against the Jews and the

Crusaders." This purging of Christians, Jews, and Hindus is going on today across the Middle East, from Pakistan, Bangladesh, and Iraq to Lebanon and Egypt.

This purging does not look like an Arab Spring; it is a shameful ethnic cleansing. Islamic intolerance of others is now directed at full force and without mercy against the Copts, the only minority left in Egypt. They were also the original natives of seventh-century Egypt before the country fell under the control of the Arab Islamic invasion. The current purging, which started with the Jews, followed by other minorities, is now being completed to turn Egypt into a pure Islamic state like that of Saudi Arabia. One minority after another has been removed. Who will be alienated and purged next? Will it be those suspected of apostasy from Islam, socialists, moderate Muslims, critics, intellectuals, the educated classes, or women who refuse to wear the hijab? Islamist hatred and intolerance have no end. Islamists have no tolerance for differences and do not intend to coexist with other groups. This intolerance is not unique to Egypt, by any means. It is simply more noticeable in Egypt because Egypt has the largest Christian population in the Middle East. Christians are threatened all across the Middle East— in Lebanon, Iraq, Syria, Pakistan, Afghanistan, and other countries. This moral catastrophe cries out for coordinated international action.

Another very disturbing trend is the rise of vengeance toward Israel. It emerged clearly on May 13 when a huge rally took place, again in Tahrir Square, in which the demonstrators openly expressed their wish for renewed hostility against Israel. Some even claimed that Ilat, the Israeli city on the Red Sea, was actually Egyptian property that Egypt needed to get back from Israel. This trend undermines the peace and stability that are necessary to establish the freedom and democracy that Egyptian protesters were eager to achieve.

The interim government recognized that the emerging power of the Muslim Brotherhood might lead to one of its own becoming the next leader of Egypt, so the government moved quickly to consolidate forces with Islamist groups, both inside and outside of Egypt. The interim government began to foster a new and improved relationship with Iran and allowed the passage of Iranian warships through the Suez Canal. It also opened the previously sealed Rafah border with the Hamas-controlled Gaza Strip, making it much easier for weapons to be smuggled in to threaten Israel. While the streets in Egypt were still on fire with hopes for democracy, the interim government had brokered a reconciliation treaty in Cairo between the leaders of Hamas and Fatah for a unity government. Egypt's new alliances with Hamas and Iran were a clearly hostile move in its "cold peace" relationship with Israel. None were good signs for peace, freedom, and democracy.

A nationalist mood has evolved, with people expressing hostilities against Israel similar to those of the Nasser era. It reminds me of my youth in Egypt during his time. Yet this new Nasserite movement has arisen around an Islamist core that could be much more radical and dangerous than the one under the Nasser regime. Islamist thugs are everywhere, threatening anyone who rebels against Islamic principles. This includes violence against shop owners who sell alcohol, even if it is to the Christian population.

The situation in Tunisia was different to begin with. It has always been a unique country in the Arab world, in its ability to reject radical Islam and maintain a law against polygamy. As a result, Tunisia has suffered through many attempts by outside Islamist groups to bring down its anti-polygamy laws.

After the country's moderate leadership stepped down, the system was soon challenged by Islamists. In January 2011, a Tunisian Islamist leader, Rached Ghannouchi, returned to Tunisia from London, where he had lived in exile for about twenty years. Ghannouchi had founded an Islamist organization in 1981 named "Ennahda," which was inspired by the Muslim Brotherhood. His arrival in Tunisia after the revolution was celebrated by thousands of people. Although the threat from Islamists in Tunisia is not as devastating as in Egypt, in July 2011 they stormed into a cinema in the capital city of Tunis to stop the screening of *Neither God nor Master*, a film that promotes secularism. Whether it is in Tunisia, Bahrain, Yemen, Egypt, or even Saudi Arabia, al Qaeda is already congratulating Islamists everywhere for giving it a great opportunity. The revolutions and the removal of pro-Western Arab regimes have empowered the terrorist movement. All Islamist groups, and they are many, believe that with the Arab Spring, there is an opportunity to revive the caliphate state, or the Ummah. Only time will tell whether they will ever achieve their dreams, but there is no doubt that the Islamist movement has benefited from and been empowered by the uprisings.

The death of bin Laden was another indicator of the force of Islamism, exposing beyond any doubt how powerful and popular Islamism is and how weak moderates are in the Middle East. As I described in chapter 1, almost no one in the Middle East rejoiced at his death, and this was the man whom many Muslims accused of having hijacked Islam and given it a bad name. The truth of how Muslims actually felt about him became obvious in the many eulogies that could be found all over the Internet. It is naive to believe that Islamist leaders have little support, when in reality they are often looked up to as heroes and are considered the vanguard of Islam. Even the most popular Arab TV station, Al Jazeerah, aired a program about bin Laden that was very respectful and complimentary, a tribute to his life. We can understand why the United States did not surrender his body to his people, because his tomb would have been made into a shrine representing Islamic triumph over America and venerating the man who brought fear of and perhaps, in some parts, respect for Islam around the world.

The inability of "moderate" Muslims to form a powerful alliance as an alternative to Islamists proves that their position in the eyes of Islam is weak and even illegitimate. There is no such thing as moderate Islamic scriptures that support peace, tolerance, respect for other religions, or loving one's neighbor or enemies. The few verses of tolerance in the scriptures have been excised by the concept of abrogation, leaving very little for moderates to use as support from the Koran when debating Islamists to prove them wrong. Moderation is only in the minds of peaceful Muslims but not in their scriptures, and that is why moderates are weak and always lose their arguments with Islamists. That is why moderates choose to live in denial and create an image of Islam that does not really exist. That is why they expect a positive outcome, and every time a revolution occurs, their hopes are built up, only to be dashed by great disappointment.

Those few in Egypt who understand the true problem do not dare speak about it. Some Egyptians pretend to be Muslims despite no longer espousing the Muslim faith, and they live under the threat of death if their secret should be uncovered. I often hear expressions of fear from my apostate friends in the Muslim world, such as this one from Egypt: "I feel extremely anxious at the out-of-control situation, the reckless violence that many are fooled into believing is justified. They are asking for renewal of hostilities and war with Israel. I do not believe they even understand the meaning of peace or war or the power of those they want to fight. They do not understand that their true enemy is Islam. Nonie, do you think I have time to escape this mess? I fear I will not leave this country alive." Another apostate told me, "The situation is borderline mass insanity. . . . I want out but cannot get a visa to a Western nation. What can I do?"

Their fears are far from groundless, especially after we've all seen how rapidly Islamists have asserted their power. Many Egyptians feel helpless at witnessing the "Talibanization" of their country, a radicalization that is believed to be not only forced on Egypt by internal forces, but also supported by Saudi Arabia. That kingdom is watching the developments in Egypt, afraid of a true democracy blossoming so close to home. A post on the Internet titled "Is the Egyptian Revolution Hijacked?" reported that at the entrance of the City Stars Shopping Center, the largest mall in Cairo, troubling signs were placed above the door after the revolution. Pictured is an image that looks like a stop sign with the figures of a man and a woman together and crossed out in the middle, indicating no mixing of the sexes. A sign next to it shows a sleeveless dress also crossed out in the middle, meaning that un-Islamic clothing is not allowed. This mall is majority-owned by the Saudi Sharbatly family, which is obviously trying to steer Egypt in the direction of Saudi Arabia. Nothing will better protect Saudi Arabia from calls for modernity, human rights, and women's rights than the radicalization of surrounding Islamic countries and making them more like Saudi Arabia.

The nascent women's rights movement in Egypt also took a nosedive when it was reported that Salafi groups in Alexandria distributed flyers ordering female residents of the city to wear head scarves when going out and threatening to "assault"—some said "kill," others said "burn with acid"— women who did not comply. As for the government, it has done nothing to punish or stop people who are distributing such threats. Instead, it is arresting and jailing bloggers who are critical of the new situation.

The protesters in Tahrir Square were but a small segment of the 80 million–strong Egyptian population, 75 percent of whom are either illiterate or semi-educated. That fact alone will put three-quarters of the population in the pocket of the Islamists, because these masses do not read Islamic scriptures and so rely on and believe what their religious leaders tell them. A recent poll conducted before the revolution found that more than 75 percent of Egyptians wanted to live under Islamic law. It is not a great leap to say that most of these Egyptians fall into the illiterate or semi-educated majority. Being pro-sharia clearly means pro-Islamism, and because they are the larger majority of Egyptians by far, it is hard to imagine how freedom or democracy will arise now or in the near future in Egypt. What makes the situation even grimmer is the fact that the remaining 25 percent includes the oppressed Christian Copts, who are 10 percent of the Egyptian population. As to the other 15 percent—those who would rather see a secular government—they have been overpowered and silenced, and, as I mentioned earlier, they dare not publicly say that sharia must be taken out of the Egyptian constitution. The possibility that Egypt will gradually turn into a theocracy similar to that of Iran is a more likely scenario.

The truth is that the Muslim Brotherhood exerts influence whether or not it is legal or in power. The Brotherhood represents true Islam in the eyes of the average Egyptian, and that is how it maintains its authority. The Brotherhood wants to enforce sharia, and that is what Islam mandates. Whether we like it or not, an Islamic state (the Ummah) is what Islamic theory aims for, with a final objective of ruling the world under a one-party Islamic Ummah. The Brotherhood's goals, in that sense, are the same as those of al Qaeda. The new interim leader of al Qaeda, Saif Al-'Adl, has credited his organization with exposing the true face of recent Arab and Muslim rulers to the Arab masses and empowering them to rise up against their oppressive regimes. He has also stated that al Qaeda is working to inspire the Ummah, to incite it to wage war, and to act as a vanguard for it in this blessed jihad to weaken the greatest idol (the West). From there on, the Ummah will rise up and liberate itself from the idols that weigh heavily on its soul (that is, the Arab rulers).

Whether it is al Qaeda, the Muslim Brotherhood, Hamas, Hezbollah, Jamaat Islamiyya, the Taliban, or even the radical Salafi sect, these Islamist groups have no problem with using violence, harsh punishment, and terror to achieve their goal, since this is allowed under sharia. Their goal is clearly stated in Muslim scriptures, and these groups take scriptures very seriously. Some are more violent than others, and some go through periods of image rehabilitation, if necessary, but what they never give up on is their divine goal.

The Muslim Brotherhood has committed violence from its inception and has attempted and succeeded in many assassinations of Egyptian leaders, creating fear and chaos in all aspects of society. It has also inspired and brought to life many other radical and terrorist groups, including al Qaeda itself.

After the worldwide condemnation of Islamist groups, especially after 9/11, the Muslim Brotherhood has found it convenient to try to rehabilitate its image so that it can rise to political power. Because other groups that the Brotherhood gave birth to, such as al Qaeda, were already doing the dirty work of terror on the Brotherhood's behalf, the Brotherhood started to promote itself as a nonviolent pro-democracy group. Even the U.S. director of national intelligence James Clapper described the group as "largely secular," disregarding its stated Islamist goal as summarized in its emblem, which has two swords (a symbol of Islamic conquests) and in its center the words *Wa Aiddou*, which in Arabic means "and prepare."[2] These are the first two words at the beginning of one of the most violent verses in the Koran, commanding Muslims to commit terror: Koran 8:60, "Prepare against them whatever arms and cavalry you can muster that you may strike terror in the enemies of Allah, and others besides them not known to you. Whatever you spend in Allah's Cause will be repaid in full, and no wrong will be done to you." The creed of the Muslim Brotherhood states, "Allah is our objective. The Prophet is our leader.

The Koran is our law. Jihad is our way. Dying in the way of Allah is our highest hope." How can anyone claim that this is a nonviolent or secular organization?

Like the Muslim Brotherhood, certain other Islamist groups are working hard to give the impression that they no longer espouse violence, but that should not fool U.S. government officials, because they have a lot of intelligence at their disposal telling them otherwise. Seemingly different Islamist groups often work like an orchestra, like a well-coordinated network, in which the level of violence of each group depends on its specific objectives in the location and the time period it happens to work in. Every Muslim country has an underground or openly operating, legal or illegal, Islamist group that wants to enforce sharia. A large percentage of the Muslim public regards the groups' members as doing Allah's work and sympathizes with them, giving them respect and power. Financial support regularly pours into their pockets from a good portion of the Muslim population, Islamic governments, and wealthy Arabs. They often do the dirty work that Muslim governments cannot do in the open. Iran is perhaps the only country that has no underground Islamist group, and the reason is simple: the Islamists are already in power. With such strong financial and moral support, Islamist groups now run an international network with branches operating openly under fictitious names in Western countries.

The enforcement of sharia is the goal of all Islamist groups, and Islamists understand that sharia leaves no room for democracy. That is why Islamist protesters in London carry signs that read "Democracy and freedom go to Hell." Not only do Islamic laws deny freedom of speech and religion, as well as equal rights under the law for both men and women, Muslims and non-Muslims, there are laws that punish sexual crimes with flogging, beheading, and stoning, and others that make the creation of a democracy virtually impossible.

Perhaps the most dangerous law in sharia that stands in the way of democracy is the one I described in chapter 1 stating that "a calipha [Muslim head of state] can legally hold office through seizure of power, meaning through force."[3] That law is the reason every Muslim leader must literally turn into a despotic tyrant to survive. When a Muslim leader is removed from office by force, we often see the Islamic media and masses accept it and even cheer for the new leader who has just ousted or assassinated the former leader. The deposed leader is often called a traitor to the Islamic cause.

A second law that will hurt democracy and peace states that performing jihad is one of the basic duties of a Muslim head of state: "To undertake jihad against enemies, dividing the spoils of battle among combatants and a fifth for deserving recipients." This is clearly stated in all sharia books. This important obligation is repeated several times: "The caliph fights all other peoples until they become Muslim."[4] In sharia, the definition of *jihad* is "to war against non-Muslims, derived from the word *mujahada*, signifying warfare, to establish the religion."[5] Muslim leaders who reject ruling by sharia and refuse to perform jihad are condemned as unfit apostates, and sharia commands the Muslim public to remove such leaders from office: "Muslims are obliged to rise up and remove a leader if he is no longer a Muslim, alters the sacred law, or makes reprehensible innovation [*bidaa*].[6] Not many people know that Sadat's assassination followed many fatwas of death against him for having violated his Islamic obligations to make Israel an eternal enemy. He became an apostate, according to sharia, and had to be killed or removed from office. Such laws can only cause civil unrest, political chaos, and revolutions.

Because Arab pro-Western leaders who want to maintain peace with Israel are the primary targets for revolutions, it is no surprise that the first two leaders to go were were the moderate ones who got along with the West. It is also no surprise that the Iranian Islamic leadership seems to be the only government that is immune to attacks from the Islamists.

There are more laws that can only produce tyrants and dictators, for instance: "It is obligatory to obey the commands and interdictions of the caliph, even if he is unjust."[7] On one hand, the Muslim public is commanded to remove a leader from office if he does not rule according to Islamic law, but on the other hand, they are commanded to obey him if he is unjust. Ruling according to sharia is more important than justice. Sharia also exempts the Muslim head of state "from being charged with serious Hudood crimes such as murder, adultery, robbery, theft, and drinking."[8] These are the laws that created the likes of Saddam Hussein and many other Muslim dictators. As long as such laws are present, democracy can never succeed.

Such laws and many similar ones give Muslim leaders the tools for despotic one-party rule. Yet at the same time, all leaders have to guard against assassination attempts and coups, which unfortunately are also allowed by the same laws that gave them totalitarian power.

Reformation of the Islamic political system is made very difficult by laws that condemn to death anyone who speaks against sharia. This includes Muslim leaders, who have no choice but to rule accordingly. Throughout history, there have been many examples of critics of sharia who ended up dead. That is why many Islamic intellectuals simply dance around the subject but never dare address it. Sharia has become the elephant in the room that everyone must put up with and never disturb. The most some people do is claim that Islamists misinterpret Islamic law and even the Koran itself. Even feminists in Saudi Arabia claim that Islam has given them many rights and privileges, but it is the interpretation that stands in the way. This game of denying clear-cut laws will not succeed in changing the reality, and Islamists know it.

As a result, Islamic activists and reformers have a very difficult job on their hands, because the true cause of tyranny, dictatorships, and instability cannot be touched, and they are left with nothing to blame except their dictators, non-Muslim minorities, external influences, Israel, or the West. Anything is fair game, except to uncover the Islamic sacred cows that support tyrannical rule.

Cosmetic adherence to Islamic rules is not enough, and that is what Mubarak learned after seeing his predecessor killed for signing a peace treaty with Israel. To prove to his critics that he takes his Sharia seriously, Mubarak, in 1991, added to the Egyptian constitution Article 2, which states that sharia supercedes any other law. Yet because he did not actually rule by it and stood against the jihadist aspirations of the radicals, he was still considered unfit to rule as a Muslim leader. That is why there were signs in Tahrir Square stating "Game over for America's Arab puppet dictatorship regimes." The phrase "puppet of the West" is perhaps the worst shaming expression a Muslim leader can be called, because it means the Muslim leader is befriending people he should be at war with.

Muslim leaders often hide their friendships with the West to avoid the devastating title of "U.S. puppet," and they go to great lengths to appear harsh and critical of the West in public, when in reality they want coexistence. That can perhaps explain the well-known two faces of the typical Muslim leader: a friendly one to the West in private and a critical one in public.

Clearly, the 2011 Muslim uprisings to overthrow dictators were not motivated only by the brutality of the tyrants; otherwise, the first ones to go would have been Ahmedinejad, Gaddafi, and Syria's Assad, not the two relatively moderate pro-Western dictators, Mubarak and Zin El Abidine Ben Ali. The removal of Gaddafi, who was among worse dictators, could have only been accomplished with the help of the United States and European forces. Without outside help, Gaddafi would still be in office. The Iranian leader Ahmedinejad is enjoying high popularity in Egypt and across the Muslim world, more than inside his own country, and perhaps that is one reason he is more secure in his position. The reason for Ahmedinejad's popularity is due of his defiance and attacks on the United States and Israel. That also explains why the new Egyptian interim government is promoting a friendlier relationship with Iran.

I am afraid conditions do not look encouraging in Tunisia, Egypt, Libya, or Syria, either. They are all prone to turning into Islamofascist states and not the open, democratic states the protesters had hoped for and expected. The future of these nations is still unclear, especially because the bloody civil unrest continues even after some of the leaders have stepped down. Other Muslim nations are watching and are discouraged from following in their footsteps, for fear the uprisings will only bring more tyranny after falling into the hands of Islamists.

Because of the lack of moral and legal foundations for freedom and democracy, I fear there is little hope in Egypt. From a more positive perspective, however, this revolution could be the first step in a long process of trial and error if Egyptians heed the examples of non-Muslim nations that rose up against tyranny and succeeded. Can Muslim countries humble themselves and learn from their own struggles, failures, and successes, as well as from those of other nations?

Freedom and democracy did not come easily to the United States, but what helped was a moral and legal foundation that did not stand in the way of change. Can the Muslim world produce, accept, and follow someone similar to a Benjamin Franklin? Will people rally around his vision and values, or will he be condemned as an apostate enemy of Islam before he can ever rise to power?

There could hardly be a greater contrast than between the Arab/Islamic culture, which rejects novelty and innovation, and the culture that produced the American Revolution, a culture that embraces a tradition of spontaneously forming civic, social, and support clubs and organizations to meet almost any need or interest. Whether it is sports, arts and crafts, literature, philosophy, scientific investigation, agriculture, or mutual assistance in times of crisis, Americans are accustomed to reaching out and trusting one another as individuals to help and be helped, teach and be taught, share, invent, debate, and network. In Islamic culture, new ideas are rejected, citizens are motivated by pride and shame, genders are severely segregated, relationships are plagued with distrust, and nothing can be accomplished except what is allowed under Islam.

After reading a biography of Franklin, I was extremely touched and fully understood the greatness of my adopted country, the United States. Its traditions go back to the earliest days of the British colonies in North America, and no one exemplified them better than Franklin, the founding father honored on the hundred dollar bill. Fifty years before the American Revolution, Franklin was a young tradesman, not an aristocrat by birth, who was organizing groups of other middle-class tradesmen to discuss any and all topics, philosophical and practical, with a key stipulation: regardless of the topic, members of the club were sworn to tolerate differences, including religious ones. Consider the questions that members of one of Franklin's clubs were asked to answer before being admitted:[9]

- Do you have disrespect for any current member?
- Do you love mankind in general regardless of religion or profession?
- Do you feel people should ever be punished because of their opinions or mode of worship?
- Do you love and pursue truth for its own sake?

I do not think the Muslim world is ready for a Benjamin Franklin. Not now, at least, because it lacks the moral foundation and equilibrium to form a free, stable, and fair political system. Looking critically at Islamic law and the Islamic model of government is still unthinkable for Muslims. Consequently, they keep moving one step forward and two backward and end up going nowhere. Muslim society suffers from amnesia when it comes to lessons from its own history, the chief one being that Islamic law has never worked and can never solve modern-day problems. With all good intentions and hope for a better future, the Muslim citizenry keeps falling victim to the same perpetual vicious circle over and over again, going from dictatorships to revolutions, as tight control over an increasingly enraged population is followed by an explosion against the system. This cycle, as clear as the sun rising every day, cannot be seen clearly by ordinary Muslim citizens, who learn only the fabricated history and information fed to them by their media and government. Thus, the search for a solution never goes beyond regime change, and tyrants keep erupting again and again. They are allowed to rule and are blessed by a divine legal system that no one dares to change and that has total control over every aspect of life and behavior.

Many in the Muslim world lack an understanding of what hinders them from developing an open democratic system. I am afraid that my brothers and sisters in Egypt are slowly but surely compromising and settling with the Islamists. They seem to be slowly embracing extremism, instead of true democracy, and thus will continue to rise and fall and stumble from one revolution to another, living under one tyrant and another, while looking for the ideal Islamic state that never was. The fourteen-hundred-year-old Islamic history of tyranny will continue unless sharia is rejected as the basis of the legal and political systems in

Muslim countries. Sharia must be rejected if Egyptians truly want democracy and freedom.

Judging from the history of Islamic revolutions, unfortunately, they are doomed to fail. The so-called Arab Spring, a flowery name for what has become a series of bloody Islamic revolutions, started as a spark of hope but will end in an out-of-control fiery conflagration. It did not take long for things to turn ugly and go back to square one, where Islamist tyranny will seize political power in Egypt, and perhaps Tunisia, Libya, Yemen, and other nations in the Middle East.

Freedom will come to the Muslim world not through physical revolutions, but through an internal philosophical and moral revolution. The next chapter will examine how the Islamic state has failed the Muslim individual and his morality and humanity.

3

A Muslim's Burden: How Islam Fails the Individual

Much has been written about the ideals of Islamic political thought, the caliphate, and sharia, but little has been written about the impact and interaction of these ideals on Islamic individuals, their character and values. Thus, it is fair to ask whether what the Muslim individual is taught—in terms of what to value and how to behave—is in harmony with the ideals of the Islamic caliphate. Will such values produce a conflicting or a consensual political culture? Has Islamic political ideology solved the problematic relationship between government and individuals in terms of their rights and duties?

To begin to arrive at an answer, it is illuminating to consider what Muslim students learn from a dominant Islamic scholar, Sheikh Abu Ishak Al Huweini, who teaches at the most reputable Islamic university in the world, Al Azhar University, the same Islamic university where President Barack Obama gave his famous speech to the Muslim world in 2009. Al Huweini said,

> The era of Jihad for the sake of Allah has come upon us; it is a pleasure to perform what Mohammed's companions competed to do. The cause of the poverty we are in today is because we have abandoned jihad. If we could conduct a jihadist invasion a few times a year, many people on Earth would become Muslims. Those who reject our dawa, "proselytize" or stand in our way, we must fight, take as hostage and confiscate their wealth, women and children. The pockets of the Mujahid will then be full with wealth when he also possess 3 or 4 slave women and children. This [slavery] can be a profitable business and a financial shelter like a commodity, to a jihadist in time of need; just multiply each slave head by 300 or 400 dirham. No one can make such profits through any other business [regular hard work] even if a Muslim goes to the West to work.[1]

When this audio of a statement he made eighteen years ago was translated into English and posted on the Internet in May 2011, Sheikh Huweini, now an enormously popular media star, went back on Egyptian TV to defend what he said then. The sheikh did not apologize for endorsing slavery as an acceptable source of livelihood or for encouraging his students to enslave non-Muslims and ransack their property and possessions as an Islamic right. What he did was reassert the legitimacy of what he had said by citing references from the Koran and the Hadith as support. Huwaini stressed that this kind of behavior—killing, raping, and enslaving—is only forbidden toward other Muslims but not against non-Muslims, and he again confirmed that sexual slavery of non-Muslim women is allowed, saying, "When I want a sex-slave, I go to the market and pick whichever female I desire and buy her and no need for marriage or papers." By citing the Koran as his source, he was able to silence his critics and enjoy the blessings and praise of his many supporters for having the courage to speak the "truth."[2]

Huweini is correct in stating that what he advocates has the backing of Islamic ideology, which supports his incitement to violent jihad, to kill, take hostages, commit sexual slavery, and steal the property of non-Muslims as a solution to the problem of poverty among Muslims. This is just one example of the kind of solution the slogan "Islam is the solution" offers up to the poor captive Muslim population. Muslims are told that waging destructive jihad and enslaving non-Muslims are more profitable than hard work and creating a productive economy. With this kind of mind-set, it is no surprise that Islamic countries are economic basket cases and that their non-Muslim minorities are suffering enormously and shrinking in numbers.

This is the Islamic ideological backing for the actions of the Somali pirates who hold ships' crews as hostage for money or else kill them. The history of marauding by Muslims goes back to the Islamic Barbary pirates from North Africa who attacked American colonial ships as early as 1625, according to documents. Europeans suffered more frequent attacks not only on their ships but also from raids on European coastal towns. The Ottoman Empire did nothing to stop the attacks, and when the Libyan ambassador was asked what law gave Barbary pirates the right to seize ships, his answer was that it was "written in the Koran."[3] The main source of income for most Islamic rulers in North Africa at that time was from the booty, the ransom, and the slaves obtained from Islamic piracy against European and American ships.

The American and European First Barbary War lasted from 1801 to 1805, and the Second Barbary War began and ended in 1815. There is also Islamic ideological support for the beheadings and the hostage taking that occur today in countries such as Afghanistan, Iraq, and even the Philippines among the Muslim minority. It is not only radical groups that are responsible. Often the kidnappers do it for money—not for ideological reasons—to sell the "heads" to terrorist groups, who later behead the hostages, on camera, to weaken the resolve and morale of the West. It is hard to believe that in postrevolution Egypt, rife with instability and civil unrest, prominent men of Allah, such as Huweini, advocate these actions.

Yet if the main objective of Islam is expansion and world domination at any cost, then preaching a get-rich-quick scheme to the foot soldiers, with Allah's blessings, makes perfect sense. That perhaps explains why Christians are being slaughtered and their wives kidnapped on a regular basis in the Muslim world today. Young Muslim men and women are subjected to this toxic value system and moral decadence from birth, by preachers, schools, politicians, and the media, some more blatant than others, but they all agree on the same goal: Islamic supremacy. Islam remains the only well-established religion today that commands the use of force as a right and a duty, promising fighters personal enrichment on earth and seventy-two virgins in heaven. Islam has elevated precepts long rejected by humanity as a proper way to live—a set of beliefs long repressed by many religions in order to allow civilization to blossom and flourish.

The values taught by those such as Sheikh Huweini pull the rug out from under the feet of civilization, undermining a state of peace and stability that the rest of the world is striving for. In the jihadist world of Islam, little or no value is given to hope for peace, trust, respect for human rights, and a positive look on humanity as a whole; only the law of the jungle can be the outcome. Values such as stealing from non-Muslims to enrich oneself have been elevated over hard work and enslaving others over the brotherhood of man. In that sense, Islam enforces on its followers a value system that promotes the dark side of humanity, where jihadist murderers are blessed by their God, while their victims are called "enemies of Allah." Alarmed Muslim friends in the Middle East are sending me e-mails bemoaning that with the rise of religiosity exhorted by Islamists, there is also a rise in bad manners, family infighting, anger, and abuse, which they believe have reached epidemic proportions. How could this be the role of any religion?

Muslim youths who suffer from unemployment, sexual frustration, and gender segregation are especially vulnerable to such teachings. They have heard no statement from an official Islamic religious authority condemning what Huweini preached, nor was there an official denouncement by Al Azhar Islamic University, which he graduated from and where he taught. The reason is indeed as Huweini

said, that what he advocates comes right from Muslim scriptures. "I have been made victorious with terror" (Bukhari:
V4B52N220). "Also [prohibited are] women already married, except those whom your right hands possess" (Koran
4:24). This means that Muslim men are prohibited from
having sex with married women unless these women are
non-Muslim captives who were forced into sexual slavery.
Islam gives the right to the captors of enslaved women to
annul their marriages and take them as sexual slaves: "So
enjoy what you took as booty; the spoils are lawful and
good" (Koran 8:69) and "He who believes in Allah and His
Messenger has protected his life and possessions from us. As
for those who disbelieve, we will fight them forever in the
Cause of Allah. Killing them is a small matter to us" (Tabari
IX:69).

After seventeen years in the Egyptian educational system
and my religious education in Islam, it dawned on me that
I was never taught values such as the brotherhood of man,
respect for human rights, pursuing peace and harmony in
our relationships with people outside our faith, and treating our neighbors, including neighboring countries, as we
wished to be treated. Such values are never taught in Islamic
culture, not even in a nonreligious social setting. It was all
about jihad, martyrdom, conspiracy theories, and hatred of
the other. The sad thing is that Muslims as a group have
never found anything unusual or bad about this—even I
never fully understood this until later in life, when I came to
live in the United States.

How can concepts such as freedom and democracy—the
concepts espoused in the "Arab Spring"—survive in such
a hostile environment? Are Tunisians, Egyptians, Syrians,

Yemenites, and others in the Middle East fooling themselves? Do the protesters fully understand that? I do not think so. The overwhelming majority of Muslims are taught and led to believe that "Islam is the solution"—the motto of the Muslim Brotherhood—and that if true sharia is applied in the way it was meant, it will bring heaven on earth to the believers.

For centuries, the Muslim mind has lived in a cultural bubble, believing in values contrary to those espoused in the rest of the world. Yet through exposure to Western culture and through immigration and modern technology, the bubble is now bursting to release extreme discontent, uprisings, and revolutions. The Islamic state is in a state of panic because young Muslims are now demanding freedoms and rights similar to those of the West, especially the United States, the staunch enemy of Islam that Khomeini once called "the great Satan." The lifestyle in the United States has become the envy of oppressed Muslims, especially the young. The obsession with Western freedoms is weakening the solidarity of the Islamic united front and its goal of turning the world into one big Islamic Umman. The Islamic state, while trying to put a lid on the youth revolutions, is racing to end the influence of Western culture and at the same time purging non-Muslim minorities within its own borders. In its panic, Islam is holding tight to protect its way of life and its totalitarian control.

Muslim leaders have long dreaded the truth being uncovered about Islam and its objective to keep the Muslim mind under total submission, which is the literal meaning of the word *Islam*. Because Islam cannot operate in a free society, it must keep control through sharia, the most barbaric laws ever created on earth, which allow a woman who sinned sexually to be buried in a ditch to her waist and stoned to death by men chanting "Allahu Akbar" (God is great). In order to survive, Islam must perpetuate tyranny and the idea that the religion is too holy to be questioned. Like the square black Qaaba in Mecca, Islamic totalitarian goals for the individual and society must remain a concealed holy secret, a mystery shrouded in black, that no one can look within or analyze. Most Muslims don't even know that the black stone they are worshipping inside the Qaaba is the same stone that pre-Islamic Arab pagans worshipped. Muslims are told to go on the Haj, originally a pagan ritual that brought wealth to Mecca, to join the thousands of pilgrims and circle around and around that black stone inside the black square structure. If one person slows down, slips, or falls, however, a stampede is almost unavoidable, causing hundreds of deaths. It happens almost annually in the Haj season.

In addition to inciting violence against non-Muslims, Islam has failed the individual in many other ways by promoting destructive values, morals, actions, and laws that are not beneficial to the healthy functioning of society. Let's take a look at some of the factors that have crippled the creation of a just, progressive, orderly society.

Exaggeration, Lying, and Slander

The biggest enemy of Islam is the truth. To promote the goal of protecting Islam and preserving the seventh-century way of life that is its basis, sharia encourages propaganda, exaggeration, distortion, slander, and outright lies. Under the title "Exaggeration," sharia states, "There is no harm in giving a misleading impression if required by an interest countenanced by Sacred Law [sharia] that is more important than not misleading the person being addressed, or if there is a pressing need that could not otherwise be fulfilled except through lying."[4] Under the title "Permissible Lying," it states, "Lying is obligatory if the goal is obligatory."[5] The same section states that the prophet said lying is permissible if it is for the purpose of settling disagreements among Muslims, in war with non-Muslims, and in the wife/husband relationship. Under the title "Permissible Slander," sharia states, "Slander, though unlawful, is sometimes for a lawful purpose, the legitimating factor being that there is some aim countenanced by Sacred Law that is unattainable by other means."[6] These three laws simply mean that the end justifies the means.

This might sound incredible, but it is condoned practice for Muslims if for the purpose of fulfilling an Islamic obligation, especially the obligation of jihad. Most Muslims have never actually read sharia laws written in support of such behavior because that is left to the *ulama*, the learned men of Islam. Muslims are always told to rely completely on the ulama's interpretation because Islamic scriptures and laws are too deep to be understood by the average Muslim and a Muslim needs a lifetime of learning in institutions such as Al Azhar University to be qualified to speak and write about Islam. Even though I spent about two years studying sharia, and most of what I write consists of quotations from Islamic books many Muslims respond not by debating me to discover the truth, but by challenging me: "Who the hell are you to speak for Islam?" As a result, most Muslims fear analyzing Islam and simply take for granted the lies of their religious leaders as being necessary and normal, especially lies to *infidels* (a derogatory word for non-Muslims), which they understand to be a crucial obligation to save Islam from the enemies of Allah who are out to get them. Yet lies invite more lies, and sharia itself allows lies not only with infidels, but also to solve disputes among Muslims and in the wife/husband relationship, thereby covering practically all relationships.

Lying to those whom Islam accuses of being enemies of Allah makes it necessary to portray them as evil and out to get Muslims. As a result, we find an entire Islamic media industry that promotes lying, slander, and exaggeration about their perceived enemies, the great and little Satans. The dread and fear of such an enemy must be revved up to a maximum level, which is the job of sheikhs and the Islamic media, to justify what Islam commands Muslims to do. Who wouldn't want to lie, rob, and steal from people who embody pure evil? It is hard for the Western mind to comprehend or believe that a religion can demand that from its followers. I have personally witnessed how Muslims are extremely offended when asked about the concept of *taqiyya*—deception in Islam. They accuse those who dare to expose holy lying in Islam of being Islamophobes. For the sake of protecting Mohammed and Islam, practically anything is allowed, and the individual Muslim is taught that protection of Islam is a sacred communal obligation that is more important than family, life, or happiness.

With its commandments to lie, slander, and exaggerate for the sake of Allah and Mohammed, Islam has burdened the Muslim with extreme shame and guilt. Why is one of the ninety-nine names of Allah the "deceiver"? How can the almighty command his creation to lie for him? How can a god sacrifice the healthy conscience of his people for the sake of expanding his influence on earth? Isn't the role of God to save his people? Why, then, is Allah commanding his people to save him? Is God trying to deceive or impress the non-Muslims of the world into believing in him? If Islam's goals are truly godly and good, then why do Muslims need to lie at all? And why is lying specifically mentioned time and again in Islamic scriptures?

Sadly, the great majority of Muslims are not aware of the existence of actual laws in Islam that command lying. I have heard my religious leaders lie, cover up, exaggerate, and define certain concepts in Islam in one way to Muslims and in another to non-Muslims. Islamic slander is perhaps most noticeable against Jews. Simply turn on Arab TV at any time, and you can watch the daily barrage of slander and outright lies, especially about Israel. Yet the commandment to slander and lie does not end there; it eventually spreads like wildfire to reach every corner of Muslim society. The phenomenon of honor killing, in which girls and women are accused of sexual crimes and killed for them, is often based not on reality, but on slanderous rumors.

Because Islam commands that some truths must be covered up, much of Islamic religious education goes unchallenged and remains vague and full of contradictions. Because of the taboos and the Islamists' extreme sensitivity to anything that appeared to go against Islam, we all nodded our heads and accepted what we were taught. The average Muslim is perhaps the number one victim of the lies and exaggerations about his or her own religion, and now leaders of the Salafi movement and the Muslim Brotherhood have united in telling the naive among the Egyptian people to trust them to bring freedom and democracy to Egypt.

Those who see the lies for what they are and dare to expose them are severely punished, and it does not matter whether they are Muslim, Christian, or some other faith. That is why if we dig down to the causes of many Islamic human rights abuses, we will find that the victims uncovered some truths that contradict what Islam states or commands. Journalists, intellectuals, artists, or inventors who refuse to go along with the lies and the sacred cows of Islam and who present new ideas that contradict the status quo are often punished severely, jailed, or assassinated, not necessarily by the government, but more often by Islamists. The bottom line is that Muslims must carry the weight of Islam's burden. The damage to Muslim society because of such laws is far reaching and causes distrust, deceit, and damage beyond our imagination.

The lying game has worked in Islam's favor for a long time, because no one wants to believe that top religious leaders of a major world religion are ordered to lie. Even though lying has benefited Islamic growth and has confused and silenced many, the command to lie, slander, and exaggerate in Islam has far more damaging consequences. It is perhaps most detrimental to the psyche of the Muslim individual, to his interpersonal relationships, to Muslim society, to the Islamic political system, and ultimately to Islam's relationship with the world at large.

Embarrassment in Translating the Koran

Many Muslim men have spent a lifetime learning the art of rhythmically reciting the Koran. The sound of their recitation is haunting and hypnotic. People who do not know a word of Arabic are captivated. That, in addition to the vague and difficult Arabic language in which the Koran was written, helps Muslims unconditionally and ritualistically accept the faith. To this day, even as a non-Muslim, I am moved by the sound of the call to prayer, "Athan." Yet translating the Koran is a very embarrassing challenge for Islam, because most of the material that is translated for non-Muslims actually condemns them to death, doom, and gloom. This is where Muslims skillfully use the right to exaggerate and lie.

The crux of the challenge comes when the literal *meaning* of what is written is examined. That is why translating the Koran from its original Arabic to other languages became a huge challenge for Arabs. It is not that the meaning is so difficult to translate or is highly intellectual, as some might claim, but that it suddenly forces Muslims to confront what is actually written in the Koran. Translating the Koran and then reading it in other languages brings it to the questioning eye of other cultures. When the rhythmic and the poetic components are removed, we are left with what should be the important aspect of any religion: the meaning. Unfortunately for Muslims, the meaning of the Koran's words is often not as easy to come to terms with as its musical and poetic recitation in Arabic.

Even today, I am very moved when I hear the Arabic recitation of Koran 3:169, which refers to those who die in the jihad for Allah's sake: "Think not of those who are slain in Allah's way as dead. Nay, they live, finding their sustenance in the Presence of their Lord." It is not the translation of this verse that brings me to tears, as much as it is the Arabic poetic verse, which reminds me of my father's funeral where it was recited as a way to comfort my mother, my siblings, and me after my father died in the jihad against Israel. Only when I read the English translation did I ask myself what it really meant to die in Allah's way and why we Muslims are guaranteed heaven only when we die in the process of battle against enemies of Allah.

The same thing goes for the verse "The Believers fight in Allah's Cause, they slay and are slain, kill and are killed" (Koran 9:11), which was never described to us as anything other than "it is our pride to die while in battle for the sake of Allah," meaning in the war against nonbelievers. In Arab culture that did not sound unacceptable, neither in the seventh century nor when I was growing up in the latter half of the twentieth century. Yet when the verse is translated, its meaning does not ring well in the ears of the non-Muslim world.

The solution for Islamic leadership is to water down the meaning, which, in other words, means to lie in the process of translating what Muslims claim to be the perfect holy book given to Muslims directly from God. A second line of defense is to assert that a devout Muslim must first learn Arabic to truly understand the Koran. When questions arise about the meaning and the translation that are not complimentary to Islam, the questioner is always accused of either misunderstanding or being ignorant of the true meaning.

Saudi Arabia has been actively trying to produce new translations of the Koran that water down embarrassing messages. It would be wonderful if the original Arabic text were revised similarly and became the new basis for Islam, but don't hold your breath. Saudis also have no problem adding a word here or there to make things appear less severe to the Western mind; for instance, many translations have added the word *lightly*, which was not in the original Arabic text of the Koran, before the word *beat,* when the Koran permitted the husband to beat the wife.

Vengeance

Vengeance is a major element in Muslim culture, and it adds another dimension to the brutality of life. Not only are Muslims ordered to lie and slander for the sake of accomplishing the goals of their religion, but they are also commanded to do holy vengeance, when the Koran says that it has been prescribed for the individual Muslim believer against those who violate or question the precepts of Islam: "O ye who believe! Retaliation is prescribed for you. He who transgresseth after this will have a painful doom" (Koran 2:178). Another verse says, "We shall take vengeance [*muntaquimun*] upon the sinners" (Koran 32:22). The word *muntaquimun* in Arabic has a much harsher and more vindictive meaning than the translation of that word to mean "punishment or retaliation." Yet another sign of how eager Muslims are to save face about what is in their books is that they actually mistranslate it for non-Muslims.

The message of Islam is clear: vengeance is prescribed for Muslims, and the word *prescribed* leaves no choice to the Muslim but to consider it his duty to be vengeful. Settling scores and inflicting pain against those who hurt Muslim individuals, tribes, or even nations was a strong cultural phenomenon in seventh-century Arabia and remains so today in all Islamic cultures around the world. When bin Laden was killed by the United States, the first thing I heard on Al Jazeerah TV was a cry for vengeance for his death.

Minding One's Business

Minding one's business and respecting the privacy of others are rare in Muslim society. The personal life of an individual is constantly under assault; one's business is everyone else's business. What you wear and eat, how you dress, whom you talk to or befriend, and what you say or do are subject to scrutiny, even punishment, by others; such punishment can range from rejection and ruining a person's reputation to physical abuse or even honor killing. This is because Islam entrusted the Muslim individual with the task of monitoring the actions of others in how they conform or don't conform to Islamic law. That can often lead some people to take the law into their own hands.

In Muslim society, a person feels perfectly justified to spy or snitch on others, from relatives to neighbors and coworkers. A Muslim individual is given too much power over fellow Muslims and is told by sharia that he will not be punished for killing apostates and adulterers. That concept of encouraging individual Muslims to police and tell on one another has transformed an Islamic state into a police state, turning brother against brother and neighbor against neighbor.

Reforming Others, Rather than Oneself

Muslims are focused on how to fix the outside world, rather than on fixing what is in their own. The Koran itself sets the example. More than 61 percent of the Koran deals with the sins of those who do not believe in Islam.

Most Islamic preaching and Friday sermons dwell on how nonmembers of the religion, the *kafir*, are evil and sinful for having rejected Islam. The Koran is full of horrific descriptions of the kafir: subhuman, inferior, unclean, apes, pigs, and deserving of mistreatment, torture, and death, all at the hands of Muslims. Yet little attention is directed to the sins of Muslims and how to nourish their souls. When things go wrong, the blame immediately is placed on the great or little Satans in the outer world who are out to get Muslims. In the eyes of Islam, Muslims earned their pride and glory, and non-Muslims earned their shame and sin.

The theory of jihad is the ultimate manifestation of a culture that does not mind its own business. Jihad is defined as "to war against non-Muslims, *derived from the word mujahada, signifying warfare*, to establish the religion."[7] Muslims will not rest until they reform non-Muslims and make them like Muslims. The fact that others do not want to act like Muslims greatly bothers the core believers of Islam. As a result, the theory of jihad, which is the core theory of Islam, is save non-Muslims from their sins by forcing Islam on them—first through inviting them, then, if that does not work, through war, terror, killing, enslavement, or heaving taxation on them, while humiliating them.

Islam exhorts its people to reform others, rather than to reform themselves, to hunt out people who don't conform to Islam; these nonbelievers are the prey who deserve every evil action. Holiness in Islam is attained by following Allah's jihad commandment, which entrusts Muslims, with their own hands, to rid the world of the sinful nonbelievers or those who reject sharia. It is not Muslim sins jihadists are looking for, but the sins of others.

Blaming Others

Taking it upon yourself to reform others implies that there is nothing wrong with you. This results in a chronic state of blaming others, a state that has reached pathological levels in Muslim society. Because of the severe and humiliating punishment that awaits sinners, Muslims are left without socially acceptable mechanisms to deal with sin, other than to hide it. Whether it is by the Islamic virtue police or vigilante street justice, Muslims are constantly reminded never to admit guilt. As a result of chronically keeping shameful behavior a secret, Muslims have developed a mechanism of denial. Actions that cause embarrassment, shame, or guilt in Muslim society are always blamed on others. "It is they who are sinners, and we are Muslims" is the theme of the Koran, which has resulted in a culture of finger pointing in which people refuse to take responsibility for their actions.

The phenomenon of blaming others is also a necessary mechanism to position Islamic jihad to the world outside Islam. "They are sinners," and the idea that we must change them and cause them to follow us by whatever means necessary is the fundamental basis of jihad. In following this line of reasoning, the eyes and hearts of Muslims are not focused on themselves but on the sinful non-Muslims. For Islamic thought to change its focus today, from that of the predator jihadist to an ideology that has respect for others and that values coexistence, would shock Islam to its core. It is very hard to imagine Islam making such a huge leap and reconciling itself with what

Allah's commandment of jihad has done to humanity at the hands of Muslims. That would be a disastrous self-revelation for Islam and Muslims, so focusing on the sins of others has become the solution for Islam. While America is immersing itself in seeking forgiveness for its history of slavery, not one Muslim intellectual or scholar has admitted to the failures of Islamic doctrine and history regarding slavery, which has never been abolished by sharia.

The Sin of Admitting Sin

Although some Muslims have resorted to their own natural instincts in dealing with guilt and sin, according to Muslim commandments, Islam warns its followers never to reveal their sins to others. Talking to others about one's wrong-doings and sins is a shameful act for which a Muslim will not be forgiven, both religiously and culturally. Mohammed said, "All of my Community shall be pardoned, save those who *commit sins openly*" (Muslim r35.1, p. 770). "It is offensive for a person who has been afflicted with an act of disobedience or the like *to inform another of it*. Rather, one should repent to Allah Most High by desisting from it at once, regretting what one has done and firmly resolving never to do the like again" (Nawawi, r35.2, p. 770). Popular Arabic sayings also support covering up; for instance, "Wa itha bulitum fastatiru," which that means if a person is inflicted with a sin, he should cover it up. Sayings of this ilk are often used as a tool of control and shame when bringing up children or to discourage unacceptable behavior, such as a young man drinking a beer in public or a young woman who admits to a friend that she has a crush on someone. Freely expressing one's feelings is discouraged, and criticism of oneself or one's family, society, or religion is in itself a sin and an admission of guilt.

Nor does Islam pardon those who repent, except for the highway robber. Sharia states, "The penalty for a crime is not obviated by the offender's having repented for it, with the sole exception of the highwayman, who is not penalized at all if he repents before he is caught."[8] Why is Islam more tolerant and forgiving of highway robbers who obviously hurt society, than, for instance, of apostates or adulterers who do not hurt society? This is another example of the twisted moral and ethical system that Muslims must live under.

Secrecy and distrust are the end result of such a warped value system, under which keeping one's distance from others can be a blessing. Secrecy has become a sign of virtue and dignity, whereas self-expression, spontaneity, and openness are signs of weakness and shameful neediness. This warped manner of adjusting to life fosters *kitman*, which means concealment, secrecy, pride, and shame. Some Muslims go as far as to unnecessarily hide most of their ordinary day-to-day activities from others, such as who visits them, where they go, and what they do with their personal time. If you say, "I'm sorry," or "Forgive me," it is often misinterpreted: you are not considered polite and considerate but instead are seen as weak, which can lead to others taking advantage of you. When I was a teenager, I remember when the mother of a close friend of mine laughingly told me that I was naive when I talked to her daughter about who was visiting us and what my family did. When I told that to my mother, she agreed and advised me not to talk to strangers about details of our life, even if I felt that there was nothing wrong in what I said.

The lesson I learned was never to trust anyone, not even with small talk about one's personal matters, because you never knew when it could be used against you.

Redemption in Islam

Almost all Muslim scholars agree that the "idea of redemption is certainly not a central one in Islam."[9] The human dilemma of finding a divine clear path that leads man to safety in the arms of God is not clear to the Muslim believer. The only guaranteed path to heaven for the Muslim is to die in the process of jihad against non-Muslims. He then becomes a martyr, a concept that is opposite to that of Christianity, where martyrdom means dying because of one's faith. In Islam, to die while fighting unbelievers is the highest act of worship and obedience to God.

Mohammed was obviously a tormented man who advocated a religion that did not provide hope, redemption, or forgiveness, neither for himself nor for his followers. Ibn Ishaq detailed Mohammed's life and actions in his *Sirat Rasul Allah*, as have other Muslim historians, documenting much murder, torture, enslavement, and acquisition of others' wealth through killing and sexual misconduct, but it is necessary to understand that the reporting of such actions was never meant to depict wrong or sinful deeds. To the contrary, these acts were portrayed as necessary actions that should be regarded as a recommended model and justifiable behavior against unbelievers for Muslims to emulate and to continue after Mohammed was gone. A good portion of the Koran and the Hadith—the sayings of Mohammed—were devoted to justifying Mohammed's violent and sinful actions. One of his wives, Aisha, commented on how convenient were some the justifications that came from Allah to explain away Mohammed's behavior. For instance, when he was attracted to his adoptive son Ali's wife, a Koran verse told him it was permissible to marry her after Ali divorced her. Afterward, Mohammed abolished the institution of adoption in Islam, and until today, Muslims are not allowed to adopt children.

Mohammed lived and died in anguish and destined his people to suffer the same, leaving a legacy of little forgiveness and redemption in Islam and of much cruelty, guilt, and confusion.

Fear of "Torment of the Grave"

Many believe that Islam's use of fear and terror is strictly directed against non-Muslims, but in reality, fear and terror are first and foremost the preferred tool that Islam uses against its own followers to bring about their compliance in the submissive society that Islam seeks to maintain. The concept of the "torment [*azaab*] of the grave" is one of the basic tenets of Islam that is taught as a motivation to believe for those who rejected Mohammed's prophethood: "So when they saw Our punishment, they said: We believe in Allah Alone" (Ghaafir 40:84).

Part of Islamic education for both children and adults is an elaborate description of what happens to the bodies of sinners in the grave. In Saudi Arabia today, young schoolchildren are taken to cemeteries to learn graphically about the torture of the grave. This kind of education is believed to be the best way to teach children to fear Allah. Islam chooses fear-based education over admitting sin and achieving redemption through grace.

It is documented that Mohammed himself was afraid of the torment of the grave. A hadith by Aisha states, "The Holy Prophet entered my house when a Jewess was with me and she was saying: Do you know that you would be put to trial in the grave? The Messenger of Allah trembled [on hearing this] and said: It is the Jews only who would-be put to trial." Aisha added: "We passed some nights and then . . . I heard the Messenger of Allah seeking refuge from the torment of the grave after this" (Sahih Muslim, V4B12N124). Note how Mohammed, though trembling with fear and guilt, was quick to accuse the Jews, not him, of being the ones who would be put on trial, only to later adopt the idea. That hadith is very telling about Mohammed's psychological state, which further explains why the Koran focuses mainly on cursing and condemning non-Muslims to doom, gloom, and eternal hell, calling them all kinds of subhuman names.

According to Islamic teachings, Allah has shielded families of the dead from torment of the grave out of mercy for the families. It is said that if God would show those alive the dead people's torment, it would be a "scandal" for the family. Even though Allah did not want the torment to be seen, the prophet gave a little peek into what goes on in the grave when he said,

> O people, this Ummah will be tested in their graves. When a person is placed in his grave and his companions leave him . . . as for the kafir or hypocrite. . . . Then a door to Paradise is opened for him and the angel says, 'This would have been your place if you had believed in your Lord. But because you disbelieved, Allah has replaced it for you with this.' Then

a gate to Hell is opened for him and then the angel struck a blow with an iron hammer between his ears and he screams a scream which everything around him can hear apart from the two races (mankind and the jinn). (Bukhari, V4 B12N22, and also Ahmad, 10577)

Other Islamic descriptions of the torture range from one's being clothed with fire, one's grave made narrow, being swallowed up by the earth, the edge of the mouth being torn to the back of the head, the head being smashed with a rock, being burned in a tandoor oven, swimming in a river of blood while being pelted with stones, and items stolen from the war booty set ablaze on the one who stole them.

Many Muslims are extremely afraid of death and often include this in their prayers: "We ask Allah to grant us refuge from the torment of the grave."

Believing in Two Opposite Views at the Same Time

A big difference between Western and Islamic cultures concerns how they each deal with contradictions. Western culture tends to apply a more objective scientific method when two beliefs contradict each other, with research being done to prove that at least one of them must be wrong. Muslim culture, however, has trained the Muslim mind to accept two opposite ideas at the same time because Islam itself has many contradictions, especially between what Mohammed advocated and how he behaved in Mecca (the first half of his message) and how he reversed himself in Medina (the

second half of his message). Because the basic commandment to a Muslim is submission, a good Muslim must accept
the unabrogated contradictions of Islam as true. Even the
way that Muslims view the prophet himself is a contradiction. One Islamic scholar described Mohammed as

> Such was our Holy Prophet Mohammed. He was
> a prodigy of extraordinary merits, a paragon of vir-
> tue and goodness, a symbol of truth and veracity,
> a great apostle of God, His messenger to the entire
> world. His life and thought, his truth and straight-
> forwardness, his piety and goodness, his character
> and morals, his ideology and achievements—all
> stand as unimpeachable proofs of his prophethood.
> Any human being who studies his life and teachings
> without bias will testify that verily he was the True
> Prophet of God and the Quran—the Book he gave to
> mankind—the true book of God. No unbiased and
> serious seeker of truth can escape this conclusion.[10]

Yet even though Muslims were taught that the prophet
was perfect, they were also taught, at the same time, that he
was merely an imperfect human being with faults like all of
us—two opposing views that Muslims must accept simultaneously. The description of his imperfection comes in handy
if someone dares to criticize Mohammed's behavior, while
the perfect image is taught as the norm. A good Muslim is
perfectly comfortable holding both views of Mohammed.

The same goes for the concepts of jihad, apostasy, wom-
en's rights, the veil, slavery, and the equality of human beings.
The confusion and contradictions are enormous, but the

tragedy is that Muslims must believe in such contradictions without questioning them in order to convince the outside world of the righteousness of Islam. What a Muslim says depends on the circumstances. Muslims can use one explanation or the other, whichever benefits Islam and jihad at that moment. How can a stable and free system come out of this?

Criminalization of Love and Beauty

Muslim society has criminalized sex outside of marriage, the celebration of love between a man and a woman, or the display of female beauty. For instance, Saudi Arabia bans any celebration of Valentine's Day, in which the celebration of love and the mingling of the sexes are not merely sins, but criminal offenses for which one can get arrested and punished. Such Islamic crimes are not enforced only by the police, but by society and the family, which often take matters into their own hands.

Within Islam, there is no elevated concept of a covenant of love between a man and a woman, because the main goal is the empowerment and expansion of Islam to achieve the caliphate (a one-world Islamic state), and everything else must come second. That applies to male-female relationships, family, and love; they all come second after jihad. Not only the government, but fellow citizens are allowed to enforce religious laws that segregate the sexes.

Distrust of Novelty and the Other

The culture of the Arabian Peninsula is by far the most ethnocentric in the world, with its obsessive battle against any influence from the outside world that might weaken the Islamic way of life. The system is especially terrified of the impact of Western culture on its followers, particularly women and youths. As a result, Islam has erected multiple barriers to preserve its laws and culture. Mohammed warned, "Beware of matters newly begun, for every innovation is misguidance" (Bukhari V3B29, p. 914). As interpreted by Muslim scholar Muhammad Jurdani, this means: "Distance yourselves and be wary of matters newly innovated that did not previously exist," in other words, any novelty or innovation in Islam that breaks the Sacred Law must be opposite of the truth, or a falsehood. This interpretation comes directly from sharia: "for every newly begun matter is innovation, every innovation is misguidance, and every misguidance is in Hell."[11] And "The Muslim head of state himself must guard the Islamic state from unlawful novelties or innovations [bidaa] that are contrary to Islamic law." That is a law that a Muslim leader must abide by.[12]

The ordinary Muslim is in a quagmire regarding whether to accept the new or anything from the non-Muslim world, because to do so may conflict with his religious obligations. Some Muslims choose hatred and aggression toward the "other," which is supported by the concept of jihad, while others conquer this predicament by allowing their humanity to rise above hate, so they actually have friendships and loving relationships with non-Muslims and borrow from their culture. Yet whatever route a Muslim chooses, no Muslim, unfortunately, can avoid a degree of guilt, especially when he or she reads the Koran and the Hadith.

Empathy and Compassion

The concept of empathy and compassion toward humanity as a whole, regardless of religion, gender, or national origin, was never a topic of discussion in my thirty years of living in a Muslim society. I have never heard an Islamic preacher dedicate a Friday sermon to this topic, except in terms of the Islamic religious duty toward orphans and the poor. Even Islamic media, politicians, and academics have neglected this topic, especially in relation to other cultures and world peace.

Because of that, Muslims in general are not aware of or do not care about the obsessive cursing and condemning of non-Muslims in Muslim books and culture. In my Muslim days, I used to listen to the weekly Friday sermons in which our religious leaders cursed the Jews and the Christians in the most cruel and vicious ways, but it never occurred to me or anyone around me or in the media that this hurt others. Christians and Jews heard these insults from the pulpits of mosques but could never protest publicly. One reason was that the Muslim public did not do anything to stop it.

We were never taught to put ourselves in the shoes of non-Muslims to imagine how they feel when they hear and read derogatory descriptions about them in our holy books. I never remember anyone defending the rights and the humanity of non-Muslims; the focus was always on the rights and the viewpoint of Muslims. Only later in life, specifically after I moved to the United States, did I start to realize how bad and unjust this was. That is when I started to speak about it, but the response I got from Muslims was not positive. It was in America, when I befriended Egyptian Jews and Christians who finally felt safe enough to talk about the torment they experienced when mosque microphones blared weekly curses at them, that I clearly saw their perspective. I was happy to hear one Muslim intellectual finally speak against the Islamic cursing of non-Muslims in a program on Arab TV about Islamophobia. Hopefully, such new ideas will start to trickle down to the Arab street and to Islamic preachers.

The Duty of Protecting Mohammed's Honor

Since its inception, Islam has suffered from a lack of self-confidence, a credibility problem. That is obvious if one reads the Koran's obsessive condemnation of those who rejected Mohammed, a man who was extremely sensitive to criticism. In the last thirteen years of his life, Mohammed tortured many people and committed merciless atrocities—killings, beheadings—against anyone who criticized or rejected him, including poets who mocked him, and Jewish tribes, as well as Arab tribes, who refused to convert to Islam. Islamic law, which was built on Muslim scriptures and the example of Mohammed, harshly punishes any criticism of Islam, and the penalty for criticizing Mohammed is especially harsh: the death penalty. These are called blasphemy laws.

Today, in a Pakistani jail, a Christian woman, the mother of five, is awaiting execution because of claims that she insulted Islam. The people who reported her to the authorities were Muslim neighbors who claimed that they heard her insult Islam, even though she has denied it. That is an example of how Islam destroys trust in one's relationships with family, friends, and neighbors, any one of whom might hand a person over to the authorities, knowing they will torture and kill people who violate blasphemy laws. That Mohammed's honor must be protected to such an extreme level is a sign that Islam cannot stand up to scrutiny. Because of its fragile self-confidence, Islam has sacrificed trust and spontaneous relationships among citizens. This is not the dignified image that all religions should project.

Muslims have inherited and internalized the tormented soul of their prophet. The more they act to silence criticism, the less they project confidence in the legitimacy of their religion to the outside world, which is what they desperately strive for. Violence is an act of desperation, and the more they use it, the more they dig themselves into a deeper hole, setting off yet another cycle of shame and guilt that they must cover up, and the cycle never ends. Because self-criticism and a debate about Islamic doctrine are not allowed, Muslims tend to be in a constant state of scrambling to cover up shortcomings, while exaggerating the faults of others. As a result, a good portion of Muslim political system, media, and preaching is dedicated to obsessive self-defense, while harshly blaming and mocking others.

After centuries of life in the Islamic mental prison, nurtured by its value system, Muslims finally find themselves facing a new shrinking world where no religion or ideology is beyond scrutiny, especially after 9/11, the loud jihadist cry on U.S. soil that exposed Islam's goals. Here the commandment to lie came in handy, when Muslims told the world that Islam had nothing to do with it and that terrorists have hijacked the religion, a denial that many in the West believed. This game must be played to ensure that the West remains confused about the true goals of Islam.

After 9/11, Muslims were suddenly caught naked in the center of the public square. The true nature of the religion they must protect from exposure with their lives is now under the microscope, and they do not like it a bit. For centuries, Islam has survived by perpetuating an image that is very different from the reality of Islam's documented history and what is in its books. The tragedy of 9/11 has been a blessing in bringing out the truth about Islam's goals toward the world. Sheikhs, who were accustomed never to being challenged in Muslim countries, are now asked on American television: "What does jihad mean?" They project a rigid, deceptive, and condescending demeanor and an inability to debate or respect the opinions of others. When they lose arguments, they resort to spin, lies, slander, and exaggeration and, if that does not work, yelling, name calling, and abandoning the discussion. Their Islamic education deprived them of a chance to learn much about other religions and sciences, and that can easily be detected when they engage in debate with pastors or rabbis who are usually highly educated in diverse fields.

The true power of the sheiks is not in their piety or holiness, but in their dreaded death warrant (the fatwa of death), which they usually delegate to some Islamist group that threatens people who defy, expose, or criticize Islam. Fatwas today are being issued against Westerners, among them cartoonists, politicians, or intellectuals who expose Islam. If you question the ordinary Muslim about those who issue fatwas, the answer is that these are simply radicals who do not represent true Islam, and many Muslims think that is all the explanation that's needed.

The more I learn about my religion of origin, the more I feel sorry for the poor Muslim individual who has to live a warped existence to survive all of the assaults on his humanity, freedom, intelligence, and happiness, for the sake of the glory and expansion of a political totalitarian ideology that is partly a religion. It is sad for me to see Islamic religious leaders, groups, and politicians be accused of promoting or being accessories to terror. Many Muslims in the West openly support Hamas, Hezbollah, and the Muslim Brotherhood and even sympathized with Osama bin Laden. Such terror groups could not be that widespread and effective without the financial support and blessing of many Muslim leaders. Many Muslims in the West are scrambling to save face, while calling those who question terrorism Islamophobes.

Such pressure has led a huge number of Muslims to be non-practicing or merely cultural Muslims. Behind the scenes and for the first time in modern Islamic history, we are also witnessing a new phenomenon. Many Muslims have found peace in leaving Islam altogether, some in secrecy, while others announce it publicly. Most of those who did it publicly live in the West, myself included, but miraculously, a few brave souls have left Islam and challenged the system from within the Muslim world.

Without America's freedom, I could never have survived or been reborn through discovering the truth that is hiding in plain sight for all Muslims to see. That truth is glaring at all Muslims, but few dare see it. The discovery process was long and hard for me. It cost me my relationship with my family in Egypt, who cut their ties with me completely, not only because I left Islam, but, more important, because I have come to love the Jewish people and support the State of Israel. That strikes at the heart of Islam's fears. The ultimate act of apostasy in Islam is when a Muslim starts to regard

Jews as equally human and worthy of love and decides that their culture, their Jerusalem, and their small nation deserve to be preserved. That constitutes the ultimate crime against Islam.

A few years ago, as I was riding in a car with a friend, I could not help but listen to the words of a song she was playing: "I'm trading my sorrows/I'm trading my shame/I'm laying them down, for the joy of the Lord." After listening to that song, I learned that a religion should not burden us with shame, pride, and fear, but should liberate us and set us free. I went home and looked at my Egyptian passport, which was stamped "Muslim" by the Egyptian government, the same stamp as on my birth certificate, my student ID, and the government ID that I brought with me from Egypt long ago. I realized that being a Muslim was not a relationship with a god, but a relationship with the state, a relationship of slave to master. Abandoning Islam is illegal in all Muslim countries, including Egypt. That is the characteristic of a religion that is afraid of the truth. The truth is Islam's number one enemy. I placed those documents back in the old box where I kept them and closed that chapter of my life forever.

It was not only the religious side of the song that captured my attention, but the idea of how a religion can free people from shame, sin, pain, and sorrow. What a difference that is from my religion of origin, where shame, sin, sorrow, pain, and sickness are all to be endured for the purpose of expanding and protecting Islam. While Muslims are all *Abdullah*, meaning "slaves of Allah," Christians are children of God. In Christianity, Jesus came to save humanity, but in Islam, it is Islam's followers who must save Islam. Jesus came to die on the cross to forgive the sins of man; in Islam, Muslims must die for the sake of Allah. In Christianity, we are taught, "We are all sinners," while Islam says, "They [non-Muslims] are all sinners." Christians bless all of humanity; Muslims curse non-Muslims. Vengeance is only God's in Christianity, but vengeance is prescribed for Muslims. Anger and envy are deadly sins in Christianity, but in Islam anger is promoted and envy is described as a curse that a Muslim must guard himself from. Islam violates practically all of the Ten Commandments, in one way or another. This might seem to be a promotion for the Judeo/Christian culture, but that is not my intent in making the comparison. The point I want to make is not a religious one, but rather how one religion can bring comfort, peace, harmony, and stability and another can be a source of the destructive force of anger, incitement, and violence.

I was finally able to open that mysterious black box I was born in, which is Islam. America gave me the key. It is now my right to examine what I was worshipping. The contents are dark, rotten, and a cover-up of unspeakable proportions. Muslims are all slaves, not to Allah, but they were enslaved to heal the pain of a tortured man, riddled with fear, guilt, and a hatred of abandonment. After Mohammed's death, Muslims had to continue his mission in blind obeisance: punishing themselves, their families, their children, and society just for the sake of destroying Mohammed's eternal enemies who dared to reject or mock him. His vengeance became the vengeance of all Muslims and his wars theirs to wage for fourteen hundred years, up until the present. Muslims have never figured out this madness, which has led to a tortured existence that has hurt and destroyed millions in jihad, not only in the Middle East, but also around the world. I was worshipping a meaningless sacred black stone that ate away at my mind, my soul, and my compassion toward fellow human beings whose only fault was being non-Muslim.

Islam fails the Muslim individual and leaves him in constant turmoil and lack of peace. While several former Third World countries, such as South Korea, Taiwan, and India, have been able to elevate themselves, progress, flourish, and achieve successful democracies, we find the Muslim world still struggling for economic survival and political stability. This drama of Islam's failed responsibility to the individual stands in the way of the Muslim developing the moral foundation that is essential to produce a healthy mind, society, and political system.

Having failed the individual, Islam has held back the Islamic mind and deprived it of growth in every area beyond vengeance, anger, paranoia, and hatred. Thus, it is inconceivable for Muslims to move beyond Jew hatred or into accepting coexistence with Israel. To the Muslim mind, accepting Jews is equal to treason against Islam and Mohammed. Why is that? The next chapter deals with why the Arab-Israeli conflict is actually an Islamic-Jewish conflict and what Israel's fears are amid the current revolutions.

4

Israel amid Islamic Tornadoes

The situation in the region surrounding Israel has long been explosive and volatile, and the recent uprisings, chaos, and revolutions have made it more so. Revolutions are by nature impulsive, and the future leadership in many Middle Eastern nations is moving toward sharia and radical Islam. Add in the threat posed by a radicalized Turkey, as well as the Iranian threat, and the volatile mix intensifies. Never before in the history of the world have more than fifty countries ganged up against a tiny state such as Israel.

The Arab-Israeli conflict has gradually evolved into an Islamic-Jewish conflict; it no longer involves only Israel and the surrounding Arab countries: Syria, Jordan, and Egypt. Even Lebanon, which decades ago had a Christian majority and kept the peace on its borders with Israel, turned against

Israel after a civil war after which the majority in Lebanon became Muslim. That was when Lebanon joined the Arab jihad against Israel. In recent years, non-Arab Islamic countries that traditionally had stayed uninvolved in the Israel-Palestine issue have moved toward a policy of confrontation with Israel. As a result, Israel's circle of hostility has now enlarged to include countries such as Iran and Turkey. The only thing that can comfort Israel is the fact that Arab and Muslim nations, which are eager to destroy Israel, are experiencing internal turmoil themselves.

The Egyptian revolution is moving in the direction of revoking Egypt's peace treaty with Israel. This trend reflects the majority opinion of the Egyptian public, as well as the will of all of the Islamist groups in the area who believed that many Arab leaders had accepted Israel. On April 25, 2011, a Pew survey found that 54 percent of Egyptians said their country should annul the peace treaty with Israel.[1]

Events following the revolution stoked the anti-Israel sentiments. Just a few days after Mubarak stepped down, the Egyptian sheikh Qaradawi, considered Islam's leading Sunni cleric, returned to Egypt. He had been in self-imposed exile since 1961, after being imprisoned several times, first by King Farouk in 1949, then three times by President Gamal Abdel Nasser. On February 18, 2011, he held a Friday prayer in Tahrir Square that was more of a huge victory rally, attended by two million people. He commanded his followers to march on Jerusalem to reclaim it for Islam.

On Friday, May 13, 2011, in another massive rally in the same square, Egyptians protested the establishment of the state of Israel that occurred on May 15, 1948. Such a protest had never taken place before in Egypt on such a scale. The crowds called on the interim rulers to end ties with Israel and threatened them with more massive protests if their demands were not met.

Even some so-called moderate leaders expressed eagerness for a confrontation with Israel. Ayman Noor, an influential opposition leader, has recently called for the peace treaty with Israel to be "reassessed." In May 2008 a well-known Egyptian blogger wrote,

> We—the majority of us anyway—don't want peace with Israel, and are not interested in any real dialogue with them. We weren't then and we are not now. The entire peace process has always been about getting the land back, not establishing better relations. Even when we do get the land back, it's not enough. People in Egypt lament daily the Camp David treaty that prevents us from fighting.[2]

Years after the 1967 Egyptian defeat, Egyptians seem to have forgotten the horrific price they paid after years of violence and wars against Israel. They seem to have forgotten their desperation and the bread riots and the food shortages after each war when they tried to get the Sinai back. Now, after Israel returned their land simply for a promise of peace, it is almost unbelievable to see that Egyptians are itching for another confrontation with Israel. Why do they believe they have a right to conquer Jerusalem? It was never part of Egypt and was never mentioned in the Koran. They got the Sinai back. Why would Egyptians distract themselves with this controversy over Israel when much needs to be done to improve their economy and bring about a democratic system? Engaging in an outside conflict or even a conflict with their Christian minority should be the last thing on Egyptians' minds. Yet that is not how the jihad culture has programmed people to think.

Islamic culture plays a continuous jihad/victimization game with the Muslim mind. That is why the likes of Qaradawi and other Islamists are inundating Egyptians with propaganda about jihad, day in and day out. Jihad is what the Islamic sense of pride, power, glory, and manhood is derived from. Egyptians are not wired to cooperate, trust one another, and dedicate themselves to the hard work of building their nation, taking care of their families, and saving their country from the rot of jihadism.

Egyptians and Arabs in general have a tendency to speak more than they act and to bite off more than they can chew. They seem to be itching for a confrontation with Israel, while the Egyptian political situation is in limbo, sectarian violence against Christians is at its peak, and the economy in shambles. Clearly, Egyptians seem to have forgotten their decades of pain and suffering and the wars with Israel, but, then, when have Egyptians ever liked to learn from their very long history?

Arab leaders who are friendly to the West and who abide by a peace treaty with Israel cannot fulfill Islamic goals. That is why the leaders of Egypt, Tunisia, and Yemen were the first to go. Hosni Mubarak was hated for maintaining ties with both the United States and Israel. For that, he was called a puppet of the CIA and Mossad. The current government of Egypt must either choose peace and be at odds with the people and Islamist groups or choose war and be at odds with the world of reason and perhaps once again lead the nation into disaster.

Right before the uprisings in late 2010, the leader of the Muslim Brotherhood, Mohammed Badie, expressed his view that "waging jihad is mandatory." In this sermon, he stated that Arab governments that stand in the way of jihad against Israel and the United States are traitors. The following are not the words of Osama bin Laden, but of Badie, whose populist group now controls the Egyptian parliament and the presidency as well:

> Arab and Muslim regimes are betraying their people by failing to confront the Muslim's real enemies, not only Israel but also the United States. Waging jihad against both of these infidels is a commandment of Allah that cannot be disregarded. Governments have no right to stop their people from fighting the United States. "They are disregarding Allah's commandment to wage jihad for His sake with [their] money and [their] lives, so that Allah's word will reign supreme" over all non-Muslims.[3]

The new Egyptian administration is finding it even harder to govern than the Mubarak administration did, because the atmosphere is out of control. The reason is that since the revolution, expectations have become unrealistically high, and many conflicting parties and views are emerging, which might be good in the long run for forming solid political parties, but in the short run, the result is chaos.

After the revolution, an Egyptian comedian joked that each Tahrir Square protestor was about to form his own political party. Soon afterward, an established Egyptian newspaper, *Almasry Alyoum*, reported that a group of Egyptians intended to establish an Egyptian Nazi party founded by Emad Abdel Sattar.[4] Could Islam follow in the footsteps of the Nazi regime's rapid expansion, only to succumb to an equally rapid and total defeat? Only time will tell. Another group has been formed that is demanding the return of the Egyptian monarchy under the son of King Farouk Ahmed Fuad II, who has been living in France since he was a child.[5]

Egyptians feel a sense of loss and are searching for their identity, something to hold onto as they decide their future. They should not even consider a confrontation with Israel if Egypt is to recover and improve, but apparently that kind of wisdom is not in Arab/Islamic genes.

Instead, the revolution is paving the way to war, not to democracy. Young democracy lovers may have celebrated over the Muslim Brotherhood's promise to create a free and democratic Egypt, but that will never happen as long as Islamism is the predominant ideology in the region. Islam simply won't allow it, and the Muslim Brotherhood knows it.

The military interim government, which allied itself with the Muslim Brotherhood, quickly became pro-Hamas, pro-Iran, and anti-Israel. The goals of Islamic governments must inevitably match the goals of the people. This should be no surprise. A poll conducted by the University of Maryland in April 2007, WorldPublicOpinion.org, found that "large majorities (of Muslims) approve of many of al Qaeda's principal goals. Large majorities in all countries (average 70 percent or higher) support such goals as: stand up to Americans and affirm the dignity of the Islamic people, push the US to remove its bases and its military forces from all Muslim countries, and pressure the United States to not favor Israel."[6] The survey also stated, "Equally large majorities agree with goals that involve expanding the role of Islam in their society. On average, about three out of four agree with seeking to require Islamic countries to impose a strict application of Sharia, and to keep Western values out of Islamic countries. Two-thirds would even like to unify all Islamic countries into a single Islamic state or caliphate."

Throughout the Middle East, from groups such as al Qaeda, Hamas, Hezbollah, Hizbuttahrir and the Muslim Brotherhood to Arab socialists and nationalist Nasserites, the goal is the same: a confrontation with Western governments, especially Israel and the United States. Throughout the Muslim world, it is a deep-rooted belief that without this confrontation, the ultimate goal—the Islamic Ummah—will not be achieved. And just as with Mohammed's example in the seventh century, anything goes in their efforts to achieve such a goal.

The prospect of a huge loss of Egyptian lives does not worry Muslim leaders. Human life is cheap in Egypt, as it is in other societies that are unable to feed their swelling populations because of dysfunctional economies. A live peasant serves as cannon fodder; a dead one is one less mouth to feed. In addition, citizens have been trained to believe in their obligation to wage jihad. As a result, they developed a macho attitude, and they never object to waging offensive wars.

Yet none of this makes sense. Renewing a hatred of Israel is counterproductive to economic progress. Peace with Israel in the last thirty years has contributed to the stability, economic growth, and well-being of both Egypt and Israel. Are Egyptians ready to throw all of that away? Unfortunately, Egyptians have made this mistake over and over. Egyptians and the other postrevolution Islamic countries seem ready to cut off their noses to spite their faces, as the expression goes, in their self-destructive overreaction to their current problems.

It is hard for a Westerner to believe that Egypt, with all of its terrible economic and political troubles, is again calling Israel its enemy. In the presidential election, many of the nominees recklessly called for the revocation of the peace treaty with Israel. Yet this is not surprising for those who understand the Islamist's deep fears and have over time seen that Egypt and Arabs in general never miss a chance to act so foolishly. The only difference between now and the past is that in previous wars the Egyptian army was trained by the Soviet Union, and in the last three decades it has been trained by the United States, a fact that might come back to bite us.

Islam has always concentrated on expanding its influence toward the outside world, more than it has on internal development. Expanding its power through intimidation, fear, and even terror counts for more than the strength that would accumulate from focusing on achievement, building admiration, and winning the hearts and minds of its followers. Islam really does not know how to break that cycle. Perhaps that is why the confused and disappointed Muslim protesters are still gathering regularly to protest in Tahrir Square. Yet now, with the international media gone, many are quietly being arrested. One video clip of protests in Cairo in late spring 2011 showed a woman holding a picture of

Mubarak, kissing it, and saying, "We are sorry." There is noticeable regret, with the nation in shock after failing to predict the power of Islamism and clarify their own confusion about what they really want.

It is thus reasonable to expect that the revolutions will produce radical anti-American regimes that will seek a confrontation with Israel. We can also assume that Israel is getting ready for the new challenge. The chaos is already spilling into Israel and will increase if Hamas gets bolder and resumes attacking Israel with rockets. Provoking Israel will naturally compel Israel to protect itself militarily, and that could bring Egypt into the equation. I don't believe that I am being an alarmist, but many Egyptians have said that they will not stand by silently if Gaza is attacked.

The primary reason for the revolutions on Arab streets was to improve people's lives, as well as the economic, social, and political systems. Yet that is not the priority of the Islamists, who want to use the revolutions to form a unified Islamist front to confront Israel and the West, paving the way for the Ummah. In that regard, Islamists are in conflict with their people's priorities and their basic need to prosper. It is true that sentiments in the Arab world are anti-Israel, but the pressing discontent of the masses is, first and foremost, economic and political. If the new radical anti-American regimes use their countries' resources for military purposes, wars, and conflicts, then the Islamic states will embark on a slippery slope of bloody confrontations, instead of the Islamist utopia of the Ummah.

It would be catastrophic for Arabs, more than for Israel, if the new Islamic leaderships rush to drag Israel into wars and conflict. The reason there is a good possibility for a conflict is that, rightly or wrongly, the Muslim Brotherhood is under the impression that they have their man in the White House, an opportunity that might be short-lived. Because Obama's reelection is not guaranteed, the Islamists will probably ignore their people's priorities and opt for an attack on Israel before the end of Obama's first term, while the opportunity lasts. I would not be surprised to see an all-out war against Israel in the summer of 2012. Israel should be ready. This time, however, if Israel is forced into a confrontation and takes the Sinai again, the Israelis should never return it.

Even if a war is not waged on Israel first, it is not unreasonable to predict bloody civil unrest arising in several Muslim countries if things get worse and not better after the revolutions. Arab rulers have always dealt with internal civil unrest by redirecting people's anger away from their government and toward Israel. Over and over, Arab governments have found that attacking Israel is an easy way to end internal conflict in their own countries, to avoid responsibility, and to deflect people's attention away from Arab rulers.

Nothing unifies the Arab world more than collective hatred for Israel, and nothing better takes the world's attention off an Arab leader's failure to get his own house in order. During the 2011 Syrian uprising against him, President Assad, right in the heat of the uprising, encouraged a large number of citizens to march to Israel's borders, knowing well in advance that Israel would naturally shoot at those assaulting its territory. It is insane, but Muslim leaders keep subjecting their citizens to certain death merely to win a few internal battles, such as, in this case, distracting citizens from internal uprisings. Yet in this instance, with the march on Israel's borders, Assad did not achieve his intended goal of ending protests against his regime.

Shooting at Israel has always been the way that Arabs solve their internal conflicts. Here is how it is done: First, Arabs must find an excuse to fire at Israel, and if they can't, they must create a reason. Stories about the latter are many, but a famous one concerned a shooting staged with the help of the media. The scene was supposed to be cross-fire between Israelis and Palestinians, without any actual fighting on the Israeli side. A Palestinian father named Al-Dura and his son were supposedly caught in the cross-fire, and the boy was seemingly killed on camera. The video does not show any blood on either person, and the little boy began moving after he was pronounced dead. French media analyst Philippe Karsenty did a heroic job of uncovering this as a hoax and embarrassed the media that promoted this video.

If staging lies does not work, then perhaps kidnapping an Israeli soldier, shooting a few missiles, or sailing a Freedom flotilla boat to Gaza will do the trick. The key strategy is to provoke Israel into shooting back. In the bloody civil unrest between Hamas and Fatah in Gaza in 2006, with the help of Hezbollah in Lebanon, both groups kidnapped Israeli soldiers and shot missiles into Israel, which led to the 2006 Israel/Lebanon war.

Arabs have mentally trained themselves to play this game without thinking, and it has often served their goals. It is unfortunate that the Western world does not seem to understand how Arabs threaten Israel's safety and security in a convoluted scheme to solve internal conflicts and manipulate world opinion so that Arabs are seen as victims of Israel.

With this strategy of provoking Israel to defend itself by shooting back at the "poor unarmed Palestinians," Arabs often kill two birds with one stone: they end the internal civil conflict, while at the same time cause Israel to be condemned by Western media and the UN. In all likelihood, future Arab civil unrest will still be stifled in the same pathological way. The manipulators do not care at all about the loss of life on either side, however much they may shed crocodile tears in front of CNN's cameras.

Egypt has the largest army in the Arab world, and some people jokingly say it is an army with a country, rather than a country with an army. It is doubtful that an Egyptian leader will actually break the peace treaty with Israel in response to pressure from his people. No one can predict the future, but if Egypt joins the hostilities against Israel, it will not be after Egypt "officially" breaks the treaty. Egyptians do not usually operate this way. It will more likely be the result of their smuggling weapons into Gaza, or perhaps Egypt will claim that Israel was the aggressor, saying that Israelis broke the treaty when they were provoked to fire back. With new blood coming into the conflict from Iran, Turkey, and Lebanon, all indications suggest that a confrontation is brewing against Israel. Then Israel will once again find itself surrounded by enemies on all sides. This would be reminiscent of the awful days under President Gamal Nasser in the 1950s and the 1960s, when Egypt's existence revolved around the destruction of Israel. I lost my father to that struggle, and thousands of Egyptian soldiers unnecessarily lost their lives.

Israel has defied all odds, survived, and thrived, while suffering through repeated terror attacks from all directions by nations that have a pathological obsession to destroy it.

Most nations would crumble under such pressure, but Israel is a truly unique country. What Israel has on its side is the truth and its conviction and faith in itself, its survival, and its purpose. The Islamic cause is a deceptive and convoluted goal that must hide its true intent, which is to eliminate an entire group of people, the Jews, for no reason other than that they are Jews.

This situation is unparalleled in human history, in its complexity and dysfunction. The true innocent victim in this drama is Israel, which represents the Jewish people in the eyes of Muslims, and which is dragged unwillingly into the Islamist web of unreasonable conflicts. At the center of all of this is Islam's deep existential fear that goes back to the prophet Mohammed and keeps repeating itself to this day.

Islam's obsession with the Jews reaches back to its origins and is part of a huge cover-up of deep shame and guilt over Mohammed's behavior toward the Jews of Medina. All of the atrocities and the violations that Mohammed committed against the people of Arabia were covered up and erased from their memory when they converted to Islam, except for one group that never accepted Islam, even by the sword. That group consisted of the Jewish tribes of Medina, who chose expulsion and decapitation over abandoning their faith to Islam. What Mohammed did to the Jews of Medina has become the unspeakable cover-up of Islam, actions that no prophet—or human being, for that matter—should commit even against his worst enemy. No prophet documented in the history of man, except Mohammed, has ever committed mass genocide.

In chapter 3, I explained how Islam burdens Muslims with the duty of protecting Mohammed's honor, an unusual demand of its followers by a religion. Mohammed's honor was stained, not by the Jews, but by Mohammed's own behavior toward them. That memory of Mohammed's shame survived in Mohammed's mind until he died, and it continues to live in the minds of Muslims as long as there are Jewish people.

One of the last things that Mohammed addressed on his deathbed was what he cared about the most. His last words were about his success in making Arabia free of Jews, Christians, and any religion other than Islam. Yet Mohammed's deathbed words did not end there and were followed by this well-documented hadith ("saying"): "The Hour [Resurrection] will not take place until the Muslims fight the Jews, and kill them. And the Jews will hide behind the rock and tree, and the rock and tree will say: oh Muslim, oh servant of Allah, this is a Jew behind me, come and kill him!" (Sahih Muslim 41:6985; Sahih Bukhari 4:52:177).

With these final words, Mohammed commanded Muslims to pursue the Jews wherever they went in order to kill them. This hadith declared the existence of an entire group of people illegal under Islam. It was a fatwa of death (a death warrant) against Jews. This hadith did not originate in recent times; it was not documented by Muslims only after Israel became a state in 1948. Instead, it was stated as a commandment by the prophet of Islam in the seventh century.

Anti-Semitism originated with Islam. This religion has launched waves of hatred against Jews in many other areas of the world.

Muslims today are still fighting the unfinished business of Mohammed. That is why the Arab-Israeli conflict should be more accurately called an Islamic-Jewish conflict, because non-Arab Muslim countries such as Iran have now openly made this conflict their own. If we look at a map of Israel in comparison to a map of the Muslim world, from Morocco to Indonesia, no sane person will believe that this is simply a Palestinian problem about land.

These are not only my words, but the words of many Islamic leaders and Islamic scriptures that state that the Jewish problem is not a problem over land. Listen to the words of two top Muslim scholars. Qatari cleric Sheik Muhammad Al-Muraikhi said, "We do not treat the Jews as our enemies just because they occupied Palestine, or because they occupied a precious part of our Arab and Islamic world. We will treat the Jews as our enemies even if they return Palestine to us, because they are infidels. They rejected Allah and His messengers."[7] Egyptian cleric Muhammad Hussein Ya'qoub said, "The Jews are the enemies of Muslims regardless of the occupation of Palestine. You must believe that we will fight, defeat and annihilate them, until not a single Jew remains on the face of the earth."[8]

Why is that? Have Muslims ever questioned why their prophet demanded them to kill Jews wherever they find them? Why do their religious leaders say they must annihilate the Jews? What could ever drive a prophet and the holy men of Allah to promote such a vendetta? A truthful analysis and answer to these questions will expose an existential dilemma at the heart of Islam. If it is fully exposed to Muslims, then I have no doubt that Islam will cease to exist.

When Mohammed embarked on his mission to spread Islam, his objective was to create a uniquely Arabian religion, one created by an Arab prophet, which reflected the

Arabian culture. Yet to obtain legitimacy, he linked it to the two previous Abrahamic religions, Judaism and Christianity. He expected the Jewish tribes who lived in Arabia to declare him their Messiah and thereby bring him more legitimacy with Arabs, especially with his own tribe in Mecca, the Quraish. Because his own tribe had rejected and ridiculed him, Mohammed needed the approval of the Jews and their conversion to Islam to prove to Meccans that they had made a mistake by rejecting him. He then migrated to Medina, a town that had predominantly been settled by Jewish tribes and a few Arabs. The Jews allowed Mohammed to move in.

At the beginning, the Koran of Mecca was full of appeals to the Jews, who were then described as "guidance and light" (5:44) and a "righteous" people (6:153–154), who "excelled the nations" (45:16). Mohammed expected that the Jews would be eager to believe in him and his new religion, but the Jews refused to convert to Islam and abandon their religion. Mohammed was alarmed, and the tone of the Koran toward the Jews changed from appreciation to warning: "I have come to you with a Sign from your Lord. So fear Allah, and obey me" (Koran 3:5). Still, the Jews refused to take Mohammed as their Messiah and pointed to his lack of knowledge and mistakes in his understanding of the Bible. Mohammed was devastated and could not control his anger, envy, and wish to punish them for humiliating him. He felt their refusal to be a great blow to his credibility and his hope of getting the respect he yearned for from his own Mecca tribe. The rejection of the Jews reinforced his tribe's belief that he was a fraud.

Mohammed then escalated his threats toward the Jews, especially after he began to feel empowered by winning battles against other Arab tribes. When his threats did not work, he described Jews as subhuman apes and beasts: "For the worst of beasts in the sight of Allah are those who reject Him: They will not believe" (Koran 8:55).

Rejection by the Jews became an intolerable obsession with Mohammed. Not only did the Jews reject him, but their prosperity made him extremely envious. The Jewish tribes were successful businessmen who earned their living legitimately, through agriculture, trade, and tool making. On the other hand, Mohammed earned his living and wealth through warfare, by attacking Arab tribes and trade caravans and seizing their wealth and property. That did not look good for a man who claimed to be a prophet.

Mohammed also had his eyes on the wealth, the homes, and the women of the Jews and wanted them for himself and his warriors. Because the Jews were the ones who welcomed him to live among them in Medina when in desperation he needed to leave his tribe, Mohammed had to find a reason to justify his attack against them. Mohammed accused the Jews of having broken a treaty, and Allah himself agreed with Mohammed in a verse of the Koran: "They are those with whom thou didst make a covenant, but they break their covenant every time, and they have not the fear [of Allah]" (Koran 8:56). There was never any proof of the Jews having signed a treaty, but still Mohammed's anger kept building up. "And let not those who disbelieve suppose that they can outstrip [Allah's purpose]. Lo! they cannot escape" (Koran 8:59). And escape from Mohammed's violence, the Jews could not.

One Jewish tribe after another was subjected to siege, execution, and confiscation of property. Mohammed's soldiers were put under incredible pressure to fight against the

Jews, among whom they lived as fellow Medina citizens. The Koran documented that some wanted to flee from the bloody battles against the Jews. Fighters who wanted to avoid killing the Jews were cursed, shamed, and called hypocrites in the Koran: "That Allah may reward the men of truth for their truth, and punish the hypocrites" (Koran 33:24). "And those of the people of the Scripture who backed them [the Jewish tribe], Allah brought them down from their forts and cast terror into their hearts, a group you killed, and a group you made captives" (33:26). The Koran here referred to the killing of the male Jews and capturing the women and the children. It is important to note that the Koran referred to Allah as the cause of the terror in the hearts of the Jews. As the Koran stated, Allah was actually the one responsible and not Mohammed. As to the property that Mohammed seized, the Koran legitimized it in Surah 33:27: "And He caused you to inherit their lands, and their houses, and their riches, and a land which you had not trodden." The Koran comforted Muslims after they seized the property and the homes of the Jews they had just beheaded, saying these were a legitimate inheritance given to them by Allah.

Islamic books that document the life of Mohammed, written by the well-known Ibn Ishaq and Tabari, detailed what happened to the Jewish tribe of Banu Qurayza, which lived in Medina, at the hands of Mohammed and his followers. Even the angel Gabriel allegedly encouraged Mohammed not to abandon fighting and actually joined him in the fight:

> Gabriel said that the angels had not yet laid aside their arms, and that he had just come from pursuing

the enemy. "Allah commands you, Oh Muhammad, to go to Banu Qurayza. I am about to go there to shake their stronghold." After being divinely inspired even by angels, Muhammad then placed the tribe under siege for twenty-five nights after which they were given the choice to follow Mohammed as Allah's prophet, or lose their lives, property, women, and children. The Jews said: "We will never abandon the laws of the Torah and never change it for another."[9]

Islamic documentation of the senseless attacks on the Jewish tribes revealed details that are hard to believe. For instance, in the middle of this siege Mohammed was concerned about whether the Jews were speaking ill of him, and it was even recorded that Mohammed and his companions approached the Jewish forts and said, "You brothers of monkeys, has Allah disgraced you and brought his vengeance upon you?" According to Islamic sources, the Jews replied, "Oh Abul-Qasim, you are not a barbarous person." Then, step by step, one can see a desperate Mohammad trying to convince his own Muslim fighters that the angel Gabriel himself was riding a white horse toward Banu Qurayza "to shake their castles and strike terror to their hearts."[10]

Mohammed was keen on not slaughtering Jews without convincing his reluctant followers that all of the decisions to kill the Jews were made jointly with the counsel of others. Mohammed picked a man by the name of Sad who understood what he wanted to do and asked him what he thought should be done with the Jews. Sad said, "I give judgment that the men should be killed, the property divided, and the women and children taken as captives." Mohammed responded by praising Sad, saying, "You have given judgment of Allah above the seven heavens."[11] First, it was Gabriel, then Sad, then Allah himself who gave permission for what followed. The Jews surrendered and were detained, then Mohammed ordered trenches to be dug. The Jewish men were brought out in batches of ten or twelve. They were beheaded and their bodies thrown in the trenches. Among them was a man by the name of Huyayy bin Akhtab, who said to Mohammed, "By God, I do not blame myself for opposing you, but he who forsakes God will be forsaken."[12] Then Akhtab told the men, "God's command is right a book and a decree, and massacre have been written against the Sons of Israel." Then he sat down, and his head was struck off. The number of beheaded adult males was estimated to be six hundred to nine hundred. The bloody massacre was completed in about two days.

The mass genocide committed by Mohammed was reported in Muslim scriptures not as a sin or as something to be ashamed of, but as a justifiable deed. Then Mohammed and his followers took the massacred men's properties, businesses, and homes. They held the women and the children as slaves. Many of the women became sexual slaves of Muslim fighters, and Mohammed himself chose one of the women for himself, Rayhana, daughter of Amr bin Khunafa. She remained his sexual slave until she died.[13] The mass theft of Jewish property and the sexual enslavement of their women were documented as follows: "So Muhammad began seizing their herds and their property bit by bit. He conquered home by home. The Messenger took some people captive, including Safiyah and her two cousins. The Prophet chose Safiyah for himself."[14]

One does not have to be an authority on human behavior to see how tormented Mohammed must have been after this massacre he conducted to empower and enrich himself and his religion. To reduce his torment, he needed everyone around him to participate in the genocide against the Jews, the only people whom he could not control. An enormous number of verses in the Koran encouraged fighting as an act of obedience and even as a method of worshipping Allah and promised fighters many rewards on Earth and in Heaven, while those who refuse to fight and fled were condemned. Muslims were encouraged to feel no hesitation or guilt for the genocide because it was not they who did it, but Allah himself: "Fight them, *Allah* will punish them by your *hands* and bring them to disgrace" (Koran 9:14), meaning those who kill are innocent of any crime because it was Allah who used their hands. Then Allah, in another Koran verse, confirmed: "when thou threwest [a handful of dust], it was not thy act, but Allah's: in order that He might test the Believers by a gracious trial from Himself: for Allah is He Who heareth and knoweth [all things]" (Koran 8:17). Allah is the one doing the throwing by using Muslim hands to test their will to obey Allah. Those who kill pass the test of Allah.

The persistent message in Islamic scriptures is that Muslims, like their prophet, are destined for war and vengeance. It has been prescribed for Muslims, and they cannot run away from it. There is an element of shame directed at anyone who dislikes war: "War is prescribed to you: but from this ye are averse" (Sura 2:212). "Fighting is prescribed for you and ye dislike it. But it is possible that ye dislike a thing which is good for you and that ye love a thing which is bad for you. But God knoweth, and ye know not" (Sura 2:216).

Mohammed never got over his anger, humiliation, and rejection by "the people of the book" (which is what the Koran called Jews), whom he emulated and heavily relied on for legitimacy. Even after all of the Jews were driven out of Arabia and even after all of Arabia became Muslim, his obsession persisted until the day he died. The mission he left for Muslims was to go after the Jews who still survived in lands the Muslims had yet to conquer.

As I wrote earlier, Mohammed's message on his death-bed was not for his followers to strive for holiness, peace, goodness, and to treat their neighbors as themselves, but a commandment for Muslims to continue the killing and the genocide against the Jews. That was the last thing on Mohammed's mind before he died. It was the shame and pain that he carried to his grave.

By asking his followers to continue the genocide for him until the Day of Judgment, Mohammed expanded the shame to cover all Muslims and Islam itself. He was not going to sin and go down alone. All Muslims were commanded to follow his example and chase the Jews wherever they went after they fled with their lives, penniless, toward their holy land or to the south to what is now called Yemen. And chase them the Muslims did. Muslims today must continue fighting, to do Mohammed's unfinished business, and they must perpetuate the cover-up of Islam's bloody shame.

After Mohammed's death, Muslims continued their expansion beyond Arabia, conquering great civilizations,

Arabizing and Islamizing them by the sword and through a system of taxation that punished non-Muslims. Jerusalem fell into Muslim hands soon after Mohammed died, and that was the Muslims' chance to fulfill Mohammed's death wish. More than one hundred years after Mohammed's death, after Muslims occupied Jerusalem, they chose to erase all memory of Jewish existence, their religion and culture, by building a mosque and calling it Al Aqsa Mosque, right on top of the ruins of Solomon's Temple, the holiest spot of the Jews. The message of Islam was "You and your history are finished." The same thing was done to the pagans' Qaaba in Mecca, after Mohammed captured and destroyed all of the gods of Mecca and declared it to be the holy land of Islam. When Muslims entered Egypt, Persia, Constantinople, India, and other lands, they did the same thing. Whether the places of worship were churches, temples, or simply holy sites of other faiths, Muslims converted many of these to mosques. The message of Islam became "We do not coexist, we replace."

Mohammed's decision to practice genocide and violence marked the day that Islam ended as a peaceful religion. Everything that he did in the last ten years of his life was dedicated to expansion through brutal force. There was no honorable justification for Mohammed's mass slaughter of the Jews and many others. That is why a good portion of Muslim scriptures is dedicated to justifying Mohammed's violence. In addition, to totally erase any criticism by his Muslim followers, back then and in the future, Muslims must share this murderous behavior with Mohammed. The persistent bloody message to kill had to cover the hands of all Muslims, angels, and Allah himself.

Mohammed's failure with the Jews of Arabia became an unholy dark mark of shame in Islamic history, and that shame, envy, and anger continues to get the best of Muslims today. It will as long as there are Jews. In the eyes of Mohammed and Muslims, the mere existence of the Jewish people, let alone an entire Jewish state, delegitimizes Islam and makes Mohammed look more like a mass murderer than a prophet. For Muslims to make peace with Jews and acknowledge that they are human beings who deserve the same rights as everyone else would have a devastating effect on how Muslims view their religion and the actions of their prophet.

Islam has an existential problem. By no will of their own, the Jews found themselves in the middle of this problem. Islam must justify the genocide that Mohammed waged against the Jews. Mohammed and Muslims had two choices: either the Jews are evil subhumans, apes, pigs, and enemies of Allah, a common description of Jews still heard regularly in Middle Eastern mosques today, or Mohammed was a genocidal warlord and not fit to be a prophet of God, a choice that would mean the end of Islam. Then and now, Mohammed and Muslims clearly chose the first worldview and decreed that any hint of the second must be severely punished. Jews must remain eternally evil enemies of Islam, if Islam is to remain legitimate. There is no third solution to save the core of Islam from collapsing; either Mohammed was evil or the Jews were evil.

Any attempt to forgive, humanize, or live peacefully with Jews is considered treason against Islam and Mohammed. How can Muslims forgive the Jews and then go back to their mosques, only to read their prophet's words, telling them they must kill Jews wherever they find them? It does not add up, if someone wants to remain Muslim. As a child, I remember once asking my teacher why we hated Jews so much, and her answer scared me when she angrily answered, "Aren't you a Muslim?" Hating and wishing the destruction of Jews has become synonymous with being a Muslim. Sympathizing with Jews became the ultimate betrayal of Islam. Very early in life I learned my lesson as a Muslim, as do all Muslim children: I learned never to ask that question again.

Instead of allowing religion to serve its followers and humanity, Islam had to dedicate itself to self-preservation above all else. Throughout history, Muslims who saw the great lie and wanted out have also realized, as did the Jews, they could not leave except under penalty of death. Islam, as personified in Mohammed, has never tolerated abandonment or rejection, and the Jews were made an example of, for every Muslim who wanted out.

Whether Muslims like it or not, they must be loyal to Mohammed, just as his fighters were coerced into fighting. Muslims today must close their minds and follow the biggest lie ever perpetrated in human history, a lie that has survived for more than fourteen hundred years and that has caused the longest and most unsolvable international conflict of today. Solving the Islamic-Israeli conflict peacefully simply means ending the legitimacy of Islam. That is why no Muslim leader can dare to seriously pursue peace with Israel without hurting Islam at the core.

Nothing shakes Islam's confidence in itself the way that Judaism and the Jewish people do, as symbolized in the State of Israel. Whether it is the Arab Spring, the current revolution, the previous revolution, Arab kings or presidents,

Islamists, socialists, moderates, or radicals, any new leadership that refuses a confrontation with Israel and the West will be condemned for committing treason against Islam and will not last. If the new leadership in Egypt chooses a policy of pursuing peace with Israel, that leader had better be prepared to be the next dictator because he will meet unbearable resistance to peace; he must imprison the jihadists and silence people who support them in the religious community. That was what Mubarak had to do.

Islam's fears of democracy, freedom of religion, and human rights are closely tied to its fear of being exposed. Allowing freedom of religion will end Islam as we know it. That is why every Islamic revolution cannot keep its promise. Islamists spin and spin and come back to where they started. Islam must continue the slander, the lies, and the hateful propaganda against their number one enemy, the Jews, and then against the Christians and any non-Muslims or even Muslims of a different sect.

Arab children in Gaza today are being taught that Yasser Arafat's death was not due to illness, but that Jews killed Arafat. Jews poisoned him, Arabs claim. In the West this kind of propaganda is ignored. But crazy Arab propaganda of today will turn into Arab reality of tomorrow. In a few decades, Islamic history and religious books could very well state as a fact that Jews killed Arafat.

Islamic revolutions today know where they are heading: they are consolidating their power for the purpose of waging jihad, not only against the Jews, but against the rest of the non-Muslim world, especially the West. It would be a fatal mistake for Western nations to think that this is only a war on Israel or that the war concerns a tiny piece of land and that Israel should give land back to its 1967 borders for the sake of gaining peace. Islam is not looking for peace. It is getting ready for a huge confrontation, and the West must stand united with Israel.

The most dangerous Islamic countries that threaten world peace today are Iran, Saudi Arabia, Egypt, Pakistan, Syria, and Lebanon, and moving in that direction is Turkey. The foreign policies of these countries are dedicated to rewarding nations and nongovernmental organizations that hurt and boycott Israel and punishing those that do not. Not one of these countries will allow any Muslim nation to make true peace with Israel, and it does not matter how many revolutions they must sustain.

In chapter 5, I turn to the new phenomenon of Muslims who have discovered Islam's biggest lie and are leaving Islam in large numbers. How Islam is treating them is not a pretty story.

5

Exodus: The Rise of Islamic Apostasy

Throughout the history of Islam, many Muslims have tried to understand, examine and reexamine, reform, adapt to, and live within Islam in peace, but most have failed. The majority have succeeded in molding themselves to the state-enforced institution of religion, with a mental image of their faith that is different from the reality of what is written in their scriptures. They live and die in the mental prison that is the Islamic state without ever realizing that religion is a matter of choice and a personal relationship with the creator.

Yet accepting life in the Islamic state was never easy for some, especially for intellectuals and free thinkers. The Islamic educational system has been especially brutal with free thinkers, forcing many to lead double lives and share their real views with only a few trusted friends. Whenever they address their work or their writing to the general public, it must always meet Islamic requirements as much as possible. The Islamic state dreads the influence of free thinkers and shields its citizens from them. It controls the impact of other faiths on its citizens by blocking their access to other religions and ideologies. Saudi educational institutions are not even allowed to teach philosophy, which encourages students to think freely for themselves and draw their own conclusions.

A poem attributed to the dean of Arabic literature, Taha Hussein (1889–1973), illuminates this dilemma. The original in Arabic, which was eloquently and beautifully written, was posted on the Internet a few decades after Hussein's death and is widely available on several Arabic websites. During his life, Hussein was accused of being an apostate (one who has renounced Islam and/or no longer believes in it, which is a capital crime under Islam). Despite the accusations of apostasy, the Egyptian government has always denied that Hussein actually converted to Christianity. The reason for the denial was probably to discourage copycats, because Taha Hussein was greatly admired all over the Arab world. Below is Hussein's poem about the Allah of Islam:

> I thought you were the misleader, who guided whomever you wished
> O harmful nourisher, who humbles arrogance and pride.
> O mighty warrior, who subtly and cleverly conceals himself.
> You cut off thieves' hands and stone women's bodies,

You establish justice by the sword, for your justice
   comes through the shedding of blood.
O creator of the fighters, tell me, where is the God of
   the weak?
If you were the creator of all, you wouldn't have forbidden some of them from surviving.
What, perchance, have you reaped from this killing
   except destruction and annihilation?
Was I worshipping a butcher, who crushes innocent
   livers?
Or was I worshipping a devil, who sent us the seal of
   the prophets?
I considered that the Garden was for the mujahi-
   deen, and the strong would live there,
With dates, grapes, figs, and rivers of wine for the
   pious.
It was the best refuge for hungry people living in the
   heart of the desert,
With beds of precious sapphire, and houris singing.
We, the lovers of the believers, came and answered
   the call.
May Allah reward you through us, for behold how
   Allah is the best rewarder.
Is your Garden strictly fighting, screaming, and sex?
You restore the previously married houri's virginity,
   and congratulate the newlyweds.
Was I worshipping a pimp, who plays with the minds
   of fools,
Or was I worshipping a devil, who sent us the seal of
   the prophets?[1]

Hussein was never physically attacked after denying his secret apostasy, but many other prominent writers and journalists have paid with their lives because of rumors that they left Islam. Egyptian novelist and Nobel Prize–winner Naguib Mahfouz survived an assassination attempt by stabbing after he was accused of apostasy. Egyptian journalist Farag Fouda was not as lucky and was killed by an Islamist vigilante in 1992. Neither of these men had announced that he had left Islam, but they were judged to have done so, based on their writings.

Many other prominent activists across the Muslim world have also been killed due to accusations of apostasy in the recent decades. In 1985, the government of Sudan executed Mohmoud Mohammed Taha, a Sudanese author and thinker; Egyptian American Rashad Khalifa, a biochemist, was stabbed to death in a Tucson, Arizona, mosque in 1990; and Ghorban Tourani, an Iranian convert to Christianity, was abducted in Iran and murdered in 2005 for the crime of apostasy. In 2007, two Muslim converts to Christianity in Turkey who ran a Bible bookstore, Nicati Aydin and Ugur Yuksel, were tortured for hours, then beheaded.

Muslim intellectuals throughout the history of Islam have had to endure mental bondage and limitations on their freedom of speech and expression due to Islamic laws on apostasy and blasphemy. A well-known example today is the British writer Salman Rushdie. Ayatollah Khomeini of Iran accused him of both apostasy and blasphemy and publicly issued a fatwa of death against him. One can only imagine how such threats hinder learning and constrict the thinking and self-expression of Muslims and their educational institutions and limit their exposure to non-Islamic arts and sciences. A quick comparison between the number of Arab and Jewish recipients of Nobel Prizes tells us a lot about the deteriorating state of learning in the Muslim world.

Many Muslim writers have recently been accused of not having the proper Islamic beliefs and of being hidden enemies of Islam who must be punished for what was termed *intellectual apostasy* by Sheikh Yusus Al-Qaradawi, a top Islamic theologian. Qaradawi warned that much of their writing demonstrates a lack of faith and

hypocrisy [which] is more dangerous than open disbelief. Intellectual apostasy is always propagated night and day. We feel its relentless and ruthless effects on our society. It needs a wide scale attack at the same level of strength and thinking. The positive religious obligation here is for Muslims to launch war against such a hidden enemy, to fight it with [the] same weapon it uses in waging an attack against the society.[2]

Accusations of apostasy and blasphemy are among the worst "crimes" within Muslim society, whether the country is considered "radical" or "moderate" by Western standards. Such accusations always arouse extreme anger, emotional outbursts, and vigilante justice against the "traitor," who is accused of betrayal and of dishonoring Islam. Islamists often use such accusations against political opponents, to intimidate free thinkers, to reject new ideas and reforms, as a weapon to silence dissent, and to keep citizens under control.

The roots of such attacks go back to Islam's origin. Mohammed was obsessed with rejection, not only by Jews, Christians, and others, but he especially hated and severely punished Muslims who abandoned Islam and said, "If someone changes his religion, then kill them" (Bukhari 26/339; Hadith 461). Mohammed was merciless with those who abandoned him personally. When, toward the end of his life, he conquered Mecca, where he originally came from, he ordered the execution of ten people, six men and four women, for abandoning Islam. He commanded that the ten must be killed regardless of any plea, even if they held onto the holy Qaaba curtain, which no one should be killed under. The message was that there should be no mercy for those who reject Mohammed.

In another instance, members of an Arab tribe by the name of Uraina suffered unspeakable torture at the hands of Mohammed when they left Medina, claiming they could not tolerate the climate (what they really meant was they could not tolerate Islam). Mohammed then sent his men after them, and they cut the people's hands and feet, branded their eyes with heated irons, and left them in the hot desert to slowly die (Bukhari, V2B24N577).

Contrary to what many Muslims claim—that Islam was spread peacefully—Mohammed forced Islam on others. Islamic historians have documented that Mohammed and a follower by the name of Abul Abbas entered Mecca triumphantly, looking for Mohammed's enemy Abu Sufian. When they met Sufian, Abbas asked him whether it wasn't time to acknowledge that there is no God but Allah? When Sufian's answer was yes, Abbas asked whether it wasn't also time to acknowledge that "Mohammed is his messenger" to which Sufian answered, "That I doubt." Then Abbas raised his sword as a threat to sever Sufian's neck and forced Abu Sufian to give *shahada*, which means affirming that there is no God but Allah and Mohammed is his messenger. Stories of this kind are never told to Muslims as proof of forced Islamization but as positive Islamic stories of triumph.

Western scholars who studied Mohammed have found that certain events in his early childhood can explain his fear of abandonment, which is clearly conveyed in Islamic writings. In Mohammed's infancy, Mohammed's mother gave him up to a foster mother, who later returned him to his mother. Yet soon after his mother took him back, she died. Mohammed's grandfather then took him in, but he also died a few years later, and his uncle raised him until adulthood. Mohammed then married a wealthy but much older woman, who died after about a decade and a half of marriage. His first wife was a great influence in interpreting his visions and the voices that he heard as proof of his prophethood. The abandonment, rejection, and deaths in Mohammed's early life are well documented in Islamic history, but Muslims have never interpreted these as the root cause of his violence later in life against apostates, Jews, Christians, and his own tribe when it rejected him.

Mohammed elevated himself to an even higher status than Allah. This is reflected in the laws of Islam, which do not automatically carry a death penalty for insulting Allah, but do carry a death penalty for anyone who criticizes Mohammed, whether the person repents or not. In that sense, Muslim scholars in general agree that apostates must be made an example of before the general public, whose members are vulnerable to corruption by the apostates' views and who might be led away from believing in Mohammed and Allah. A prominent Moroccan scholar, Sheikh Abdul Bari Az-Zamzamy, described the danger:

> Apostasy causes a total disruption and confusion in the Muslim community, and thus, a severe punishment [death] was set for it to deter anyone from thinking of it. It was originally put into force following the Jewish conspiracy against Islam. The details of that conspiracy were simply mass conversion to Islam and then mass apostasy. The main ill aim was to cause confusion and to lead people astray. Thus, the punishment was set as a precautionary measure to stop all these offenses.[3]

Mohammed's anger and merciless violence against those who rejected him forced almost all of Arabia to convert to Islam so that he would spare their lives. As soon as Mohammed died, however, a large majority (about 70 percent) of the people of Arabia quickly abandoned Islam. This was disastrous news for Mohammed's caliphs (those who succeeded Mohammed in commanding the Islamic state), who were preparing to pursue Mohammed's plan to conquer wealthy neighboring civilizations such as Egypt and Persia. Before Mohammed died, he had sent letters to the Byzantine emperor and the Persian king, warning them, "Islam Taslam," meaning they should embrace Islam to be safe. Incidentally, before 9/11, Osama bin Laden demanded the same from the United States; following in the tradition of Mohammed, he told Americans to accept Islam or suffer the consequences. Unfortunately, the Western news media did not understand the meaning of the threat.

The apostasy of the majority of the tribes in Arabia led Mohammed's successors to wage several brutal wars, called *"ridda* wars"—meaning "apostasy wars"—which lasted for two years. The followers of Mohammed won the wars and succeeded in bringing all of the Arabian tribes back to Islam by the force of the sword. Mohammed's successors could never have been able to conquer and expand throughout the Middle East without first unifying Arabia itself. Through killing and torturing apostates, Islam was able to grow. Islam's very survival relied heavily not only on violent jihad toward the outside world but, more important, on the death penalty for apostasy; on the commandment to lie, exaggerate, and slander; and on giving conflicting and dual answers to Islamic controversies and embarrassments.

The Islamic sword is literally being held to the neck of every Muslim. Beheading by the sword is the preferred manner of execution in Saudi Arabia today for those who commit the crimes of apostasy, adultery, and many other sins forbidden by Islam. The Saudi flag itself proudly exhibits the Islamic sword as a symbol that threatens the use of force in spreading Islam outwardly and keeping Muslims in line inwardly.

Not only is the legal right to kill apostates given to Islamic governments, but Islamic law allows Muslims to execute apostates unofficially by delegating this authority to individuals or groups that can operate with impunity and with no oversight from the government. This works well for Islamic governments that want to appear respectful of international human rights laws. Such a trick is known to all Muslims in so-called moderate Muslim countries, which still kill and threaten apostates in many creative ways that can be even more torturous than government executions. Muslim parents are often forced to execute their own apostate children, and, if they refuse, their own lives are threatened.

The same dynamic works in the concept of violent jihad, where Muslim governments play the same game. They try to appear to be against terrorism against the West, but they coddle and protect terrorists and finance and encourage terrorist groups to attack the West. Yet if the West asks them whether they are "with us or against us," their answer is always "We are with you and against terrorism." Such duplicity was made clear to the West when bin Laden was living in Pakistan with the knowledge and protection of the authorities. The U.S. government and the media do not fully expose the duplicity of Islamic governments in supporting terrorist groups; they only blame al Qaeda. This leaves the majority of the American public in the dark about the depth of the threat the United States is facing.

Similar to Islamic fighters who kill non-Muslims, killers of apostates are not only forgiven under Islamic law, but, as Mohammed said many centuries ago, they will be rewarded in heaven: "So, wherever you find them, kill them, for whoever kills them shall have [a] reward on the Day of Resurrection" (Bukhari, V9N64). This is the same promise that Mohammed gave his fighters when they hesitated to kill the Jews of Medina.

The Islamic death sentence for apostates applies whether the apostate is in a Muslim country or elsewhere. Mosques and the Muslim community in the United States have rejected and even threatened Muslims who criticized jihad after 9/11, along with accusing them of apostasy. This may explain why most Muslims were silent.

As a former Muslim, I understand the anguish and fear of those who leave Islam—even the ones who live in Western democracies. Many suffer from abandonment by their families, shaming, harassment, abuse, beatings, and even murder. A common theme they all voice is "We are constantly looking over our shoulders," because they are aware of the existence of Islamic sleeper cells in the United States and rumors of Islamic squads, especially in Europe, whose mission, in part, is to keep Muslims in line.

Living in the West does not guarantee people protection against punishment for leaving Islam, but it is certainly much safer than being an apostate in the Muslim world. Despite the danger that I and many others face in the United States, I thank my lucky stars every day that I am a U.S. citizen. My family in Egypt—my mother, brother, sisters, cousins, aunts, and uncles—who are not radicals, have all abandoned their relationships with me, except for one cousin and a niece.

There is no doubt that apostates in the West are living under enormous pressure from those who issue fatwas of death (death warrants) against them from inside the Muslim world. Such fatwas are a form of psychological terrorism by the same radicals who want to terrorize the United States. On page 126 is a photocopy of a fatwa of death issued by Al Azhar University in Arabic against an Egyptian man and his son, who left Islam and now live in Germany.[4]

Al Azhar University fatwa of death against an apostate in Germany.

Muslim leaders today can no longer contain their fear about the growing numbers of people becoming disillusioned with Islam. This topic was recently openly discussed in the Arab media. The site aljazeera.net published an interview with Islamic cleric Ahmad Al Qataani, who expressed deep fears: "In every hour, 667 Muslims convert to Christianity. Every day, 16,000 Muslims convert to Christianity. Every year, 6 million Muslims convert to Christianity."[5]

I think his claim that 6 million Muslims convert to Christianity annually is an exaggeration, but we can never know the exact number, because most converts do so secretly. Yet there is undoubtedly a strong movement to silently leave Islam, perhaps a few million people annually. The apostasy movement today is unprecedented in Islamic history, ever since the seventh-century Riddah Wars were won by Muslims.

The recent exodus out of Islam is no longer exclusively made up of intellectuals, but now includes average Muslims. They are leaving Islam to embrace other religions, especially Christianity. The attacks of 9/11 accelerated this exodus, because it forced many Muslims to reevaluate their religion and what it really says. They have seen how it has not led them to a loving God but to desperation, ignorance, chaos, poverty, and war.

Although Muslims assert that Islam is the fastest-growing religion in the world, they fully understand that such numbers are inflated and are not due to Western infatuation with Islam, but instead to the high birthrate of Muslims. Another reason that, statistically, Islam appears to be spreading rapidly is because apostates and nonpracticing Muslims are also counted as Muslims.

The courage of former Muslims was bolstered in 2008 by the public conversion of a prominent Muslim journalist in Italy, Egyptian-born Magdi Allam, who was publicly baptized by Pope Benedict. Allam said,

> I asked myself how it was possible that those who, like me, sincerely and boldly called for a "moderate Islam," assuming the responsibility of exposing themselves in the first person in denouncing Islamic extremism and terrorism, ended up being sentenced to death in the name of Islam on the basis of the Quran. I was forced to see that, beyond the contingency of the phenomenon of Islamic extremism and terrorism that has appeared on a global level, the root

of evil is inherent in an Islam that is physiologically violent and historically conflictive.[6]

The plight of former Muslims in the West drew the world's attention when in the summer of 2009 a seventeen-year-old Muslim girl in Ohio, Rifqa Bary, ran away from home. Her father had threatened to kill her on discovering that she had secretly converted to Christianity. Her family mosque, Noor Mosque, had uncovered the story of her conversion and warned her parents to do something. When Rifqa's father threatened to kill her, she was forced to seek refuge at a church in Florida. Her family, with the help of the Council on American Islamic Relations, fought her in court for several months, after which she lived in a foster home until she turned eighteen. During Rifqa's legal and emotional ordeal, she also received death threats from her home country of Sri Lanka.

Rifqa's story was a wakeup call for me and other former Muslims in the United States. We felt that something had to be done, because we could not stay silent while our children became victims of honor killings or were forced to run away from home after facing death threats for not behaving as good Muslims should. I got together with other high-profile former Muslims in the United States, including Ibn Warraq, Wafa Sultan, Walid Shoebat, Kamal Saleem, and others. We decided to form a support group that we called Former Muslims United (FMU), to stand up and expose the Islamic threat to our lives and its violation of our basic civil rights as U.S. citizens. Wafa Sultan, in particular, had been moving from one apartment to another and spent a lot of her own funds paying for her security. The time was ripe to say,

"Enough is enough." The time had come to publicly post the e-mails we received, telling us, "You must be destroyed," or "You will be killed just like the Jews you support."

Thanks to Rifqa Bary, FMU was established in 2009. The first thing we did was ask for the support of Muslim leaders in the United States, who have the power and the connections to enact reforms and force change. We then mailed more than 165 letters (the "Muslim Pledge for Religious Freedom and Safety from Harm for Former Muslims") to various Muslim leaders and establishments in the United States. We needed their support and for them to prove how dedicated they are about reforming the radicals whom they believe are not true Muslims and who are threatening us. The pledge states that they repudiate the laws and the commandments that condemn apostates to death and discrimination under Islam. Yet unfortunately, no Muslim group operating in the United States has signed our plea letter or even responded. Only two Muslim reformists signed the pledge and are themselves accused of not being good Muslims.

Instead of support, we were attacked for being Islamophobes. Muslim leaders in America deny that there are any threats on our lives and safety. On September 24, 2009, two days after we mailed our pledges, Sheila Musaji, the editor of the *American Muslim*, wrote an article stating, "We live in a country where such freedom [of religion] is a foundational principle and must be defended. We must continue to insist on the Islamic principle that there is 'no compulsion in religion.'" She forgot to mention that this verse was an early statement in the Koran that has been abrogated by later commandments to kill apostates. Musaji, who has declined to sign our pledge, is an educated Muslim and should have been fully aware that all Islamic scholars have rejected "no compulsion in religion" as a basis for Islamic law. These scholars have relied on commandments in the Koran, on hadiths, and on the example of Mohammed to justify killing apostates.

Musaji and other Muslim leaders who refused to sign our pledge are practicing Islamic deceit with brazen confidence when they say they personally do not approve of killing apostates, which is in stark opposition to a basic tenet of Islam, the religion their organizations are promoting in the United States. Americans are especially vulnerable to such spin, which no other religion engages in to this degree. If one were to ask a Catholic, for instance, what the Vatican position on abortion is, the answer is clear. Even if people disagree with the Vatican, they will say that Catholicism does not allow abortion. Yet Muslims in the United States seem to teach, at least when it suits them, religious principles that stand in stark contradiction to the core ideology of Islam. Such double talk and lies about what Islam is has worked in favor of Islamic expansion, spreading confusion about the goals of Islam and effectively silencing people who disagree.

How can Ms. Musaji defend her refusal to sign our plea for respect for our civil rights while claiming that Muslims in the United States are speaking up against injustice and extremism? Where are the Islamic marches against 9/11? Where are their protests demanding abolition of the apostasy and blasphemy laws that condemn us to death? Where is their condemnation of the imprisonment and the death sentences used as punishment for blasphemy and apostasy today in Islamic jails across the Middle East? Where are their letters demanding the release of a Pakistani Christian mother of five who is awaiting execution in Pakistan for insulting Islam? Where is Islamic outrage over honor killing and the stoning of women for sexual sins, practices that are prevalent today in the Muslim world? How can they deny all of that? Instead, they are busy trying to spread a destructive and totalitarian religion in the United States.

Muslim groups in the United States are guilty of a disconnect from reality when they deny what is clearly a daily assault on basic human rights by mainstream Islam in the Middle East. While these groups call us Islamophobes, we in the United States are watching Arab TV condemn us to death. Just recently, Sheikh Youssef Al-Badri, a member of the Supreme Council for Islamic Affairs in Egypt, went on national TV and said, while reading from the Koran, "God has commanded us to kill those who leave Islam." The interior minister of Egypt at that time agreed with the sheikh and was quoted in a newspaper as saying, "Converts are to be killed." The majority of Islamic scholars, as well as the Egyptian public, agree with them. This video was posted on the FMU website. What more can we do?

The truth is that Muslim groups in the West are strangely silent about, and defensive of, Islamic persecution, torture, killing, and imprisonment of apostates, women, and non-Muslims all over the Islamic world. All they care about is pacifying the American public and convincing people that sharia is compatible with democracy and that Islam is a religion of peace. Whenever Western Muslim groups are asked about what is happening in the Muslim world and its tragic impact on the West, they accuse those who question them of being racists who need sensitivity training to understand the true peaceful nature of Islam. They force and shame Americans into believing there is nothing to fear from Islam. They expect Americans to reject their gut feelings that something is intrinsically wrong with Islam for causing so many Muslims to repeatedly engage in terrorism all over the world. They want us to disregard those who issue fatwas of death against Western politicians, cartoonists, filmmakers, apostates, and practically any one who dares to ask difficult questions about Islam.

Muslim apologists often speak from both sides of their mouths. On one hand, they assure Americans that Islam does not condemn apostates to death. On the other hand, they assert that anyone who announces publicly that he or she has left Islam and states the reasons for leaving has committed treason. Since the worldwide condemnation of Islamic tyranny, many Muslim countries have found a way to work around the law of apostasy: they still kill apostates but say it is for a different reason, for committing treason, rather than apostasy. It is true that as long as a Muslim keeps silent about his apostasy and behaves as if he is still a Muslim, he is left alone, but that is because no one knows about his apostasy. Yet the minute he starts to attend a church, all hell breaks loose. The person is arrested for disturbing the peace, for causing *fitna* ("divisions"), and for treason. That is the modern way of killing apostates inside Egypt.

Apparently, Ms. Musaji's seemingly more tolerant views are a form of adaptation to U.S. laws until her dream of Islamizing America is accomplished and the ugly reality of sharia becomes the law. Incidentally, on her website, Musaji has a map of the United States with the Arabic Islamic words "in the name of Allah" pasted on the center of the map.

What we have in the United States are a few Muslims arguing that the Koran does not teach violent jihad and execution, while they ignore an entire Islamic civilization of 1.2 billion Muslims living under sharia, laws that command the execution of apostates, supported by a long recorded history that details the genocide of thousands of apostates and the killing of millions throughout history by violent jihad. Both views simply cannot be right. Muslims living in the West are playing a con game with Americans.

I am in contact with several people who left the Islamic faith and either became atheists or converted to Christianity and who still live in Muslim countries, ranging from Morocco to Malaysia and everywhere in between—Egypt, Syria, Bahrain, Iraq, Jordan, and Pakistan. All of them have kept their rejection of Islam a secret, except for three pioneering individuals in Egypt who are now on the run. They have challenged the legal system that criminalizes apostasy. They are Naglaa Al Imam, Mohammad Higazy, and Maher Al Gohary. Like many others, they have been beaten and tortured in Egyptian jails, but when Amnesty International and other human rights groups questioned the Egyptian government about their situation, they were let go. Al Imam tried to get U.S. and Canadian visas to leave the country but was rejected, Higazy is in hiding, and Al Gohary eventually managed to escape from Egypt with his daughter.

I receive a good number of e-mails from secret apostates across the Middle East who plead with me to help them get out. I want to honor these people by mentioning what they wrote but without revealing their identities. Most of these e-mails came to me in English, and I translated some that were sent in Arabic:

Pakistan: "Please help me, I've got to get out! I'm a Muslim and I left Islam and please, brothers, help me out from the prison of Pakistan."

Morocco: "What you predicted happened to me. I was attacked with serious injuries, stabbed by several men on the street who shouted at me "Kafir," they definitely wanted me dead. I still wonder how they knew that I was an apostate! Maybe they saw me befriending Christians or perhaps I left my computer open on my job. I am lying in my hospital bed and the doctors told me that I was lucky to have survived. During my interview with the police I did not mention that my attackers called me "Kafir," for fear the police themselves will take notice and finish me off. I desperately want to get out but cannot leave till I am healed."

Malaysia: "Can I keep my real name a secret? I also renounced Islam. I converted into Islam in 2009 because I had a relationship with a Muslim man and converted because I was afraid to lose him, but he dumped me anyway. I really don't know what to do! I felt so stupid and full of anger. Then I realized that I was wrong to convert into Islam and I decided to go back to being Christian. I wanted to confess it to the officials, but I was afraid. I don't know where to turn to. So I decided to do it quietly. I still wore a headscarf when I went to work. When my friends asked me to join them for prayer, I gave excuses like I'm having my menstrual cycle. I was so devastated because I really wanted to tell everyone that I don't want to be a Muslim anymore. I couldn't focus on my work. I felt like I was going crazy. In the end, I decided that I couldn't continue living in lies like this anymore. Early 2010, I made my confessions at the Department of Religious Affairs. I wanted to make my renouncing of Islam official. But I was turned down. You can check into hotel Islam any-time, but you can never check out."

India: "I am Khalid from India. I am a member of a hard-line Muslim group (a well known terror group that I had to join for my security) and they don't know that I hate Islam because if anyone knows I will be dead. I love Israel and believe that it is the best country in the world. Sir, so please guide me to how to serve Israel from here in India. A servant of Israel."

Somalia: "I am a former Muslim from Somalia. I want to express my thoughts and opinions about my journey and horrible ideology of Islam, but I cannot due to my safety. How can Former Muslims help us? In other words, if I/we cannot refute and criticize Islam without hiding, how is it possible to come out and reveal the destructive nature of Islam? We cannot survive like that pretending to be Muslims, pray and act like Muslims when we are not."

Saudi Arabia: "I must be extremely careful not to use my real name. I am originally from Saudi Arabia and have family in the Gulf. I am currently in the USA and ter-ribly afraid to go back. I have converted to Christianity and ever since I have become Christian, I started having brotherly feelings towards all non-Muslims."

United Arab Emirates: "Nonie, God bless you very much. I read some of your words to the Jewish and American people, and I love what God is doing with your life. This is my story: My parents were from Egypt but I was born in the United Arab Emirates. I was born as a Muslim. . . . I grew up filled with hatred and revenge. . . . I was waiting for the time when I could sacrifice myself in the name of Allah. . . . [A]ctually my name in Arabic means Self-Sacrifice and was given to me by a Palestinian nurse who worked at the hospital where my mother gave birth to me. I was waiting for a chance to explode myself . . . killing MILLIONS of the infidels Jews and Christians. . . . it would be nice if I could explode myself many times to kill more as my Allah desired. But thanks to God. I never got the chance; until Jesus came into my life . . . but to acknowledge Jesus into my life is what I can never dare do. It is OK to kill evil infidels, but I can never know Jesus. My religion told me I could live as a time bomb. It's very simple; just study the Koran, and try to hear Allah's voice to kill. Anyway, when the September 11, 2001, terrorist attack happened, I was working as an air-hostess for an Arab Airline. I was shocked to see the massive killing of innocents' lives. And the funny thing, that was my dream to kill. . . . [B]ut Jews . . . not Americans . . . because I loved America and Michael Jackson! But the way the aircrafts hit and exploded in the two towers . . . the way they collapsed . . . it was horrific. . . . [T]he hand of Allah is seen . . . Allah is working, killing, and shedding blood. . . . I was very angry with Allah. I was thinking about the airline hostesses who knew that they would die in seconds. The people of America lived with security, peace, and freedom until the ugly hands of the greatest crafty deceiver (as Allah calls himself in the Koran). This is how we Muslims are programmed, to see the dark side of life. That's when my life changed. Now I do not have to hate, take revenge, kill, and destroy with no mercy all the infidels . . . etc. . . . Islam is not a religion . . . actually . . . it is a political plan. When I told my family about the changes that happened to me, they rejected me and I had to run away. I went to Greece and met a Christian man, but no church dared to marry us because they were afraid of Muslims. Finally, we found one brave priest who married us. Now God put in my heart much love for the JEWISH people. Every time I hear the news I get sick. There are too many lies about them . . . hatred . . . revenge. The world and Americans need to know the truth about Islam. . . , we need to help the Jewish people. I am blessed to find the truth. Thank you, Nonie, my Christian name now is Maria."

Iran: "My name is———and I am a former Muslim and an atheist from Iran. I am 28 and I have been pretending to be a Muslim for many years now (because you know what the penalty of apostasy is!). Even when I travel outside of Iran I am still terrified of saying I left Islam. Do you think that it is safe when I am in the US to say that I am not a Muslim anymore? There are many threats even outside of Iran, but I am really tired of pretending."

United States: Dear Nonie, I read *Now They Call Me Infidel* and was truly touched. I desperately need your advice. I am 26 years old, female, live in the US, an engineer and have a good job. I too no longer believe in Islam but my family, Muslims from Jordan, insist that I can only marry a Muslim man and arranged for me to go meet him in Lebanon. I am desperate, and as you probably know we Arabs must live at home till we marry, so I still live at home, and my relationship with my brothers and mother is very tense, to say the least. I must leave home, since I can no longer function even at my work, am depressed, and can't find support or anyone to talk to."

Yemen: "Miss Nonie, I was rejected to get scholarship to America. Those who were picked by the government were the radical Muslims. Meanwhile, students like me who are not radical are not getting many opportunities. I cannot live like that any more."

Algeria: "I am an Algerian man who left Islam and afraid to stay in my country. I seek the Israeli nationality."

Malaysia: "I am from Kuala Lumpur. Life is miserable and confused in the Muslim world. I cannot be a Muslim any more. I wish I could be in your position, because you finally migrated to the US and became free. I can't get the visa to America. I was very disappointed. Living in the Muslim world is quite difficult because you feel that people are always watching you for anything that might be wrong or bad against Islam. I don't understand why such radical Muslims want to kill each other and kill the infidels and blame everything on the Jews!"

Iraq: "I am from Iraq and hope to befriend Israelis and go live there because I am no more a Muslim. How can I get the visa, we do not have embassy?"

Afghanistan: "I am 23 years old from Afghanistan. I am Muslim, but I am tired of Islam. I want to see Israel and I want agreement Yahood [which means Jews] religion. Sorry I can't speak and typing English well. Please help me I want to have nationality Israeli."

Libya: "I am libyan guy. I'm not free in libya. I know more nice news about Israel. I wish leave libya to Israel but its so hard. I need help me how I can go to freedom country (Israel). I am 32 years mechanical engineer."

Pakistan: "Please help me, I am 22 years old Muslim from Pakistan, I want to marry with a Jewish girl/woman (widow/divorced) from any country because I want that my children should be Jew by birth."

West Bank: "I was born Muslim Palestinian, but I came to realize the lies and the grand deceit of the Muslim faith. I believe and trust the Living God of Israel, and there are no other gods."

It is sad to say that most of the desperate former Muslims who live in the Middle East are unable to get a U.S. visa. One educated physical therapist who spoke excellent English called me recently to tell me that his visa request to the United States has been rejected. He said that while waiting at the U.S. embassy, he noticed that a number of bearded Muslim Brotherhood types had been approved, and some of them even had marriage contracts with American women. He told me he was scared for America and wondered how such Islamists were allowed to go to the United States and he could not.

I have also been contacted by several apostates born and raised in the United States or Europe, who have converted into and then out of Islam. These once ordinary Americans have also received threats and are scared. It is estimated that about three-quarters of Americans who convert to Islam eventually leave it after a year or two. This is what one American woman told to me about leaving Islam: "I wore the Islamic garb with a sense of pride and defiance. The initial enjoyment of my Muslim husband's attention soon turned into resentment of his total control of everything I did. In the mosque I noticed that I could not touch certain topics or feel at ease asking questions. Self-censorship soon crept into my mind. But when I developed the courage to ask, I often received misleading answers. I was told that Islam honors women, but when I asked about the commandment to men to beat their wives, I was told that this is just a misunderstanding and misinterpretation of the Koran and that it really meant that men cannot hurt their wives. When I asked about the commandment to kill those who leave Islam and non-Muslims, I was told that Allah's wisdom does not necessarily appear to us humans and that Allah never commanded violence against anyone and that what I hear is a lie. I found myself asking questions in my mind but not verbalizing them to others in the mosque. How can a god say something but really mean something else? And how can He make a statement in one verse, then say the opposite in another?"

That woman, who is now a friend of mine, has left Islam and her Muslim husband and has gone back to her family and community after years of fear and threats. The death sentence for apostasy is in the early stages of creeping into American society. We must never allow it to infect the United States with the devastating tyranny it wields in other parts of the world.

Most Muslims in the West claim that Americans must not judge Islam by the fringe actions of terrorists. Western Muslims call terrorists "not true Muslims" or say that they "hijacked Islam." Yet this argument is disingenuous because Muslim society and governments are perfectly capable of stopping such "fringe" activities in the same way they are capable of stopping apostates. Claims that Muslim society is unable to suppress terrorist groups seem unrealistic and hypocritical, especially when compared to its ability to crush and subdue any Muslim who wants to leave Islam. If Muslim society treated its terrorists the same way it treats apostates, the world would have no Islamic terrorism problem.

On one hand, violent jihadists inside the Muslim world are running around organizing themselves and are unafraid of anyone, neither official Islamic leadership or ordinary Muslim citizens on the street. Islamic governments rarely threaten their lives, unless they turn against the government itself. Terrorists are treated as good Muslims. On the other hand, apostates are treated as if they have committed treason against Islam. While apostates are never allowed to form organizations or congregate, terrorists have offices all across the Muslim world and under fictitious names in the West. Something is very wrong with this picture, and it does not reflect well on Islam.

Some apostates try to solve the dilemma of Islam by trying to positively affect their Islamic communities. Keeping their apostasy a secret, they try to reform Islam from within, while they secretly do not believe in it. Although their intentions are good and arise out of genuine love for Muslim people around the world, their arguments often ignore reality. I know several of them in the United States and the Middle East. Their viewpoint doesn't make sense when they say, "We must find a way out for 1.2 billion Muslims by reforming Islam for them even though we do not believe in it." Articles are written that are critical of their logic, such as one about an "Islamic reformer who detests Islam." They continue insisting that Islam is so entrenched in many communities around the world, and they took it upon themselves to reform it, even though they no longer believe in it. I respect their efforts, but I find it difficult to believe that the reformation of Islam will come at the hands of secret apostates, who deep down in their belief system have disdain and anger toward Islam. Despite their efforts, most of them are accused of apostasy anyway.

I also know a number of Muslims who are trying to reform Islam by applying Judeo-Christian values to it. For example, they use the expression "I will pray for you," which is not at all a Muslim one. I never heard Muslims in the

Middle East tell one another, "I will pray for you." Yet in the United States, Muslims are adopting it from Christians, whom they describe as infidels in their prayers. I find that efforts to copy Christianity and Judaism in an attempt to reform Islam are disingenuous and a continuation of Islam's copying from other religions in order to get legitimacy, something that Mohammed tried and failed to do since the inception of Islam, leading Muslims into a cycle of envy and cover-up. As a former Muslim myself, I believe that the job of reforming Islam must be left to true believers in Islam. Apostates' efforts to reform Islam are simply placing bandages on the wounds. I would love to hear the leaders of Al Azhar Islamic University in Cairo declare that it is time to bring back the concept of *ijtihad* (making new laws in sharia to fit the new reality). Centuries ago, it became illegal to change sharia laws based on this concept, but without reestablishing it, there will be little hope for a reformation.

Apostates from Islam can be of great use in America's war on terror, because they do have America's best interests in mind. Former Muslims are fighting for their lives and religious freedom and want to serve the United States, the country that literally saved their lives.

As for Taha Hussein's plea in his poem earlier in the chapter, "O creator of the fighters, tell me, where is the God of the weak?" leads me to ask Allah, where is the God of the physically weaker sex, the women? Who will enlighten Islamic culture with respect to the humanity and dignity of women? How can the Islamic state be just and balanced when its laws oppress half of the population? Could the anger on the Arab streets be partly attributed to the oppression of women? The next chapter will delve into just that topic.

6

Will the Arab Spring Usher In a Feminist Movement?

So far, the Arab Spring has not rejected sharia in its constitution, and that is not good news for the rise of feminism in the Islamic state. In fact, Tunisia, Libya, and Egypt have all embraced sharia. During and for a brief time after the Arab Spring, I felt a spark of hope when I heard reports of Saudi Arabian women—albeit only a few—driving on the streets of Saudi cities in defiance of the law and subjecting themselves to severe abuse and punishment. That they were fully covered, except, of course, for their eyes, by their traditional burkas made a striking image. Yet my spark of hope was short-lived.

In response to the question "Where are the Egyptian feminists?" a number of young female college students in Egypt who understand that Islamic sharia is the problem urged a million women to march in Cairo's Tahrir Square. On March 9, about two hundred to three hundred women showed up, another sign that there is no substantial grassroots feminist movement in Egypt or anywhere in the Muslim world. The women were attacked, groped, beaten, and called prostitutes by men in the square. The Islamist women who were present did not support the students. Then the Egyptian military arrested about twenty of the student organizers and subjected them to more beatings and even—as some claim—electric shocks. A senior Egyptian military official admitted that the girls were forced to take virginity tests in order to prove they were not prostitutes, and finally they were all sentenced to one year's probation.

The Arab Spring provided a moment in which the rattled governments of the Middle East opened a window of opportunity for a few brave souls to rise against institutionalized gender segregation and discrimination against Muslim women and to demand equal rights under the law. Unfortunately, however, for serious change to take place, the majority or at least a large presence of Muslim women should have supported their brave sisters in Egypt. That did not happen. As for Saudi Arabia, the law there has not changed, and, again, it was probably because only a few elite women defied the no-female driving laws. If every Saudi woman who can drive had joined her sisters on that same day of defiance, perhaps that law could have been changed.

Change can come about when support for it reaches a grassroots or popular level, and, unfortunately, that did not happen during the Arab Spring. Why is that? How could the female citizens of the most oppressive antiwoman system on the face of the earth fail to take such an opportunity to change their destiny and that of their daughters and grand-daughters? The answers to these questions are very complex and part of the larger problem of Islam itself.

Many believe that Islam's treatment of women is gradually undergoing reformation and that it is just a matter of time before Muslim women will wise up, figure out what must be done, and stand together in unity to march for their equality and human rights. That's what happened in the West, so why not in the Middle East?

I wish it were so straightforward, but the situations are not the same. A major difference is that in the West, the Judeo-Christian value system was not accompanied by thousands of pages of Jesus's laws that demanded total submission and obedience from every Christian under penalty of death. Jesus did not tell a husband he could have up to four wives, could keep sexual slaves, or had the right to abandon and beat his rebellious wives. Jesus never called women *toys*, *slaves*, or *deficient in intelligence* and *lacking in religion*.

With all of its imperfections, the early Christian church never imposed a Christian state that forced citizens to comply with Jesus's lifestyle. Christianity did not have a holy law that condemns to death any Christian who leaves Christianity or reject its laws. Very simply, Western feminists were not confronted with the many dead ends that the Muslim feminist confronts. Compared to Muslims, Western feminists had it much easier, because the core of the Western value system allowed their emancipation. Many Western feminists might disagree with my assessment, but I have arrived at this perspective from personal experience, having lived the first half of my life in the Muslim world and the second half in the West.

There are some who believe that the defeat of sharia and the reformation of Islam will come at the hands of its most oppressed group—the women. That seems to be a logical conclusion, but I disagree that Muslim women can do it alone. One cannot expect the prisoner to be in charge of her own release when the guards of her prison are often Muslim women themselves.

For centuries, Muslim women have molded their lives to adapt to sharia and its prison, which has resulted in many having grown comfortable hiding behind their burqas. In many cases, they have created a warped mechanism of coping with a system that treats them as juveniles who need the permission of male family members to travel, to tell them whom they can befriend, and even whom to marry. When Muslim women open the Islamic scriptures, they read that women have half of the value of men, are deficient in intelligence and religion, and are not to be trusted or entrusted with too much responsibility. For instance, Sharia prohibits a woman from becoming a head of state or a judge. Her testimony in court is half the value of a man, and the explanation is that she is forgetful and needs someone else to remind her. Muslim scriptures state that women are slaves, possessions, and toys to their husbands and even that women are like dogs in distracting a man. For Muslim women to rise up against what Islamic holy books and laws condemned them to be, they must criticize sharia, which is an act of apostasy in itself. Expecting Muslim women to be behind the reformation of Islam and sharia is like asking slaves to end their own slavery without the approval of their masters or asking prisoners to get out of prison without the guards opening the doors.

Some people point to me and other former Muslim women who speak out as evidence that there will be reform in Islam. Yet women such as Wafa Sultan, an outspoken American author of Syrian origin, and Ayan Hirsi Ali, a Somali Dutch author and feminist, along with myself and others, have given up on reform after years of failing to reconcile our basic human rights, freedom, and dignity as women with the religion we were born into. The fundamental tenets of Islam are built on the submission of all Muslims, especially women. It is thus impossible to give women and even men their human rights without discrediting Islam itself or leaving a watered-down version of the religion and stripping it of its tenets of sharia, jihad, and an ambition to rule the world. To do that will end Islam, and Muslims know it. That was the conclusion that we and many other former Muslims have reached. The reason we are having some impact is less because we are women and more because we are apostates who have openly pointed at the cause of the problem, which is Islamic tyranny.

Many Western thinkers, sociologists, and analysts are baffled by how entire cultures have developed societal institutions based on the sadistic oppression of others. In Muslim cultures, this has risen to a whole new level, where misogynist cultures have managed to camouflage their cruel oppression of women in a religious package as a commandment from Allah. Violent ideologies, such as the Islamic jihad doctrine, are terrified of granting people basic human rights, especially women, because a healthy woman produces a healthy family whose members will eventually reject aggression and unnecessary violence. Women are the cornerstone in civilizing and taming male aggression, which would undermine what Islam is all about. In that sense, the freedom of women strikes at the heart of Islam and the jihad culture, and that is why feminism and Islam can never reconcile.

This does not mean there are no brave and strong women in Muslim society. To the contrary, the brutality of Islam has produced some of the sharpest, most aggressive, and persistent women in the world. Yet Islamic feminists have incredible obstacles to overcome, the most important of which are accusations of apostasy if they criticize sharia. That is one reason they find it extremely hard to develop a grassroots movement and bring on board a majority of the population. A Muslim woman's inferior status in Islamic society is too deep and is intertwined with all Islamic institutions. For Muslim women to simply revolt against this inferior status would be regarded as an act of subversion that is antiman, antifamily, antireligion, antigovernment and, worst of all, anti-Allah himself.

Women who defy sharia or try to change it are harshly attacked and silenced, and they end up withdrawing from the scene altogether or even leaving their own countries. Ghada Jamshir, a human rights activist and a feminist from Bahrain, who spoke out against female child marriage, was the victim of a government-imposed media blackout and was forbidden to write, give interviews, or talk to the media. Egyptian feminist Nawal El Saadawi had to leave Egypt after a radical demanded that her arm and leg be amputated, according to sharia. Even the influential Jihan Sadat, while her husband, Anwar Sadat, was in office, was silenced by Al Azhar Islamic University when she attempted to advocate some mild women's rights reforms.

Islamists admit that the attacks against feminists are conducted partly to make an example of them for any woman who dares to follow in their footsteps. In 2008, a popular twenty-five-year-old Saudi feminist blogger who used her real name, Hadeel Alhodaif, was rumored to have been murdered by the Saudi authorities, charges that are denied. The Saudi authorities had earlier arrested and detained Alhodaif without issuing any charges. She later fell into a coma, was taken to the hospital, and died there, but there was no report on what caused the coma.

Another huge obstacle that Muslim feminists face is the difficulty in connecting and reaching out to other women, especially the poorer and less-educated majority. Isolation in their homes, distrust of strangers, and social taboos are major factors in Islamic gender-segregated societies that restrain women's relationships, even with one another, and prevent them from organizing, especially for feminist causes. One qualification of being a good Muslim woman is that she stay in her home. Her husband will often object to her befriending activist women, and this also draws criticism from other family members and society because it is regarded as rebelliousness against Islam. Many Middle Eastern Muslim husbands hand-pick their wives' friends and often limit the women's communications only to family members.

When I was a child, I remember hearing a conversation between my mother and some other women at our house, when one of the women burst into tears, complaining about how her husband, a well-to-do doctor, forbade her to have anything to do with a woman who had been her best friend since childhood school days because of rumors that she was a feminist who wore bathing suits on the beach. The two old friends sometimes met in secret like criminals. The frightened woman said she had to be careful, because if her husband found out that she was still seeing her girlfriend, he could lock her in the house or even divorce her. What is horrifying in these situations is that society is on the side of the husbands. Often these husbands receive calls from people—women and men—reporting that their wives are being disobedient. This happened with two women my mother knew, and the whole situation ended up as a family disaster.

When I visited Egypt in 2001, I dared to wear a one-piece bathing suit with a towel wrapped around my waist at a Mediterranean beach west of Alexandria. The educated wife of a doctor in the group I was with, who was covered from head to toe, went out of her way to be rude to me. Clearly, it was because I was in a bathing suit. When my American-born daughter asked me, "What is wrong with this woman?" my answer to her later that day was, "The reason, sweetheart, is something you will never believe, because you were born and raised in America." In this case, it was a Muslim woman and not an Islamist man who tried to shame me because I was not covered up on the beach.

The only feminism allowed in Islam is that of the militant Muslim woman wearing her Islamic garb with pride and promoting sharia, the very law that oppresses her. The only way for a Muslim woman to gain respect, power, and dignity is through compliance and submission to Islam. In other words, she can earn her dignity and pride by accepting her bondage.

I have great respect for the few Arab women's rights activists who don't give up and who do what they do while living in the Middle East. They must choose their words very carefully and never openly challenge sharia. To avoid being accused of apostasy, they blame women's oppression on the misinterpretation and misunderstanding of Islam. This might help them get some cosmetic issues improved, such as, hopefully, allowing women to drive in Saudi Arabia, but with this strategy, which I can understand, they cannot change actual laws that discriminate against women. The laws are stupefying to Westerners: women receive half of the inheritance of men; women have no freedom of movement or travel; polygamy and pleasure marriages are allowed for men; divorce can occur only at the behest of men; a woman's testimony in court is given only half of the value of a man's; child marriage is allowed for girls; community property is not permitted between husband and wife; the husband is given automatic custody of the children after age seven in the case of divorce; no alimony is given to women after a divorce; a woman who is raped is required to provide four male witnesses; wife beating is permissible under the law; a husband is forgiven for killing an adulterous wife; the honor killing of women and girls is permitted; and, in some Muslim countries, the circumcision of women is allowed.

Because of blasphemy and apostasy laws that forbid anyone to speak against or criticize Islam and sharia, feminists end up dancing around the issues without hitting the bull's eye or getting concrete results. I probably would be doing the same thing myself if I were still living in the Middle East. That is the problem Islamic feminists must grapple with today.

So it comes as no surprise to see Arab women blaming the oppression of women on ignorance of the true and tolerant Islam. Former Kuwaiti parliamentary candidate Aisha Al-Rashid said, "The early Muslims were more fair and just than the Muslims of the twenty-first century. We live in the modern Era of Ignorance, I'm sad to say."[1] She is an

example of Middle Eastern feminists who must blame anything but sharia, the Hadith, *sunnah*, or the Koran.

Similar statements were made by Saudi women's rights
activist Wajiha Al-Huweidar, who also insists that Islam was
originally respectful and liberating to women and was only
later corrupted:

> Preachers spread distorted notions about women. . . .
> This Saudi patriarchal culture has become prevalent
> under religious guise, but if you examine everything
> that goes on in this society, none of it has anything
> to do with religion." She added, "How can it be that
> people are stripped of their individual judgment, and
> the Commission [for the Prevention of Vice] is sent
> to spy on people in the streets, and to determine who
> errs and who acts properly? Who gave them the right
> to do this? People have the right to decide for them-
> selves what they do and don't want.[2]

The answer to her question "Who gave them the right to
do this?" is that Islam and sharia gave the Islamic government
and its virtue police such rights. Yet it is not only the govern-
ing authorities who are the problem. Arab feminists, who
blame preachers but ignore sharia, must also ask, Where do
these preachers who spread distorted notions about women
get their views? We cannot simply say that they are all mis-
interpreting the Koran, because they are not. In fact, they are
following the Koran; they are repeating what Mohammad
and the Koran have commanded them to do. The sexual and
physical abuse of women in Islam became institutionalized
as a reward for men who wage jihad; that is the link between

women and jihad. Women have been reduced to the status of seductive sexual objects, virgins, toys, and slaves who distract men from performing the duty of jihad and of sacrificing their lives on earth for a promise of many virgins in heaven. Muslim women must compete with all of the virgins in heaven to keep their men right here on earth.

Islamic feminists have an insurmountable barrier to climb, and very little is understood about the dynamics of Islam that led to this tragedy. That is why the few Islamic feminists seem to be running in circles, only to achieve minor changes that barely scratch the surface of the problem. They have done so while paying a heavy price, earning disrespect and threats without being taken seriously. Even more sadly, their example has produced a group of Muslim women who embrace another solution: if you can't beat them, then join them. They have discovered that the key to power and respect in Muslim society is to become as radical as, if not more radical than, men. We have all seen Muslim women in black, showing nothing but their eyes, while demonstrating in London. They carry signs protesting British laws, supporting sharia, and warning Europe about another holocaust and another 9/11 to come. Sharia enforcers are pursuing a policy of generously rewarding women who tell the world that women are happy under sharia, and many embrace jihad with open arms. We have all seen Arab mothers celebrate the deaths of their jihadi sons and volunteer their other children for jihad. I do not know what is in the hearts of these women, but mothers who did so in Gaza were highly respected and rewarded handsomely with life pensions. One mother was even elected to a position in the Palestinian parliament.

An extreme and almost laughable case of pandering to sharia occurred in mid-2011 when a Kuwaiti woman, Salwa al-Mutairi, spoke to the *Kuwait Times* demanding the reestablishment of sexual slavery. The woman, who is an activist and a former candidate to the Kuwaiti parliament, wants the return of a law based on sharia that permits men to buy and sell non-Muslim girls, captured in jihad, as sexual slaves in order to protect Muslim men against seductive sexual immorality. Al-Mutairi suggested the minimum age of fifteen for non-Muslim slave girls, Christian, Jews, or other, to be sold. She demanded the immediate establishment of slave agencies—similar to agencies for maids—where the slave girls would earn a whopping 50 Kuwaiti dinar monthly and in return they would cook, clean, take care of the kids, and be the slaves of the wives during the day. At night, the girls would serve as concubines to the husbands.

The sad truth is that under Islamic law, everything Mutairi said is allowed. Sexual slavery was official and legal not only in the seventh century, when it was practiced by Mohammed and his fighters, but as recently as the early twentieth century under the Islamic caliphs. Even my own grandmother, who is half Turkish, remembers the institution of the harem existing in the Islamic caliphate. It was a way of life for some men who could afford to have and support sexual slaves. According to Islamic values, owning a slave against her will for sex and for housework is not morally corrupting, but for a man or a woman to have a loving sexual relationship with a boyfriend or a girlfriend outside of marriage is corrupting. It is especially unacceptable in Islam for a woman to have consensual sex with a lover before marriage. For that, she could be severely punished, flogged, or killed.

Unfortunately, Mutairi is not the only one who advocates the official open return of sexual slavery. Some Islamic sheikhs have spoken about their right to indulge in sexual slavery on national TV in Egypt and elsewhere. A female expert on sharia once stated on Egyptian TV that under sharia, it is permissible to rape Jewish women.

What Mutairi advocates is indicative of the pathology and the warped thinking that some Muslim women have fallen prey to, while attempting to adjust to the system. It has been documented that in Saudi Arabia, the Gulf states, or anywhere that sharia permits it, a good number of Muslim women accommodate the existence of a sexual relationship between their husbands and their maids, who are considered sexual slaves under the control of the home. Cases such as this have been discovered right here in the United States, where, in one instance, a Saudi man who pursued this lifestyle was sentenced to jail for enslaving his maid. In Saudi Arabia, he would have gone unpunished. Not so in the West. Here, the man was punished, along with his wife—as an accessory.

In the United States, there were two high-profile kidnappings for the purpose of sexual slavery: the cases of Elizabeth Smart and Jaycee Dugard. The abductors succeeded and went undetected for many years because their deranged wives were willing enablers who posed as mothers to those poor girls. Their enabling was similar to the role of most Muslim wives who accept the sexual enslavement of maids by their husbands, a situation found in many homes, especially in Saudi Arabia. Mutairi represents the worst in women: those who sell out their gender in order to gain honor and attention in a Muslim world that gives them no respect. The entire Islamic culture has succeeded in pitting women against one another and has normalized the pathology of women accepting the enslavement of other women.

Convincing Muslim women to be on the side of sharia has even reached as far as U.S. academia. Islamic and Middle Eastern studies departments in the United States have a good number of Muslim female professors who defend the veil as "liberating." In an article titled "Veil of Ignorance," Leila Ahmed, the author of *A Quiet Revolution*, wrote, "The veil, once an emblem of patriarchy, today carries multiple meanings for its American and European wearers. Often enough, it also serves as a banner and call for justice—and yes, even for women's rights."[3]

"Ignorance" in the title of Ahmed's article obviously refers to the American people who need to remove the veil over their eyes to see how liberating the Islamic veil really is. This is the kind of pride in bondage that the Islamic state has convinced many women to live by. For Ahmed and those who share her viewpoint, even the veil, an established symbol of Muslim women's slavery and oppression throughout the history of Islam, has been turned into a positive sign of freedom. What Ahmed is trying to say is that many Muslim women are wearing the veil not necessarily for personal religious reasons, but to make a statement to the outside world (a banner) to demand justice. But what justice? And if they are demanding rights in the United States, what rights is she talking about? The West is the only country to offer freedom and dignity to Muslim women, even to those who defy Western culture by wearing Islamic garb. The happiest Muslim women on earth today are the ones who are living under the U.S. constitution and the Bill of Rights.

Some Muslims in the United States claim that they have been discriminated against after 9/11, but I believe that claim is unfounded. I, an Arab and a former Muslim, have never been discriminated against in the United States after 9/11, and perhaps it is because I did not celebrate but rather mourned that day with my fellow U.S. citizens. Arab and Muslim Americans who originally came from the Middle East should know better, because compared to the Middle East or any country on earth, America is the most tolerant, welcoming, and forgiving nation. Just imagine what would have happened if nineteen American men had flown commercial airplanes into buildings in Riyadh or Mecca, Saudi Arabia. When one Danish cartoonist drew a picture of Mohammed, the entire Muslim world, governments and media, erupted with extreme anger and violence. Muslims did not say that they must not discriminate against all of the Danish people. Instead, Muslim crowds set the Danish embassy on fire, boycotted Danish products, and sent death threats to Danish people and businesses. There was no understanding on the part of any Muslim entity that this was only one cartoonist who had freedom of speech under his country's laws and who did not represent all of Denmark.

American female Muslim students who wear the hijab to protest injustice in the United States (which is the only kind of feminism allowed by Islam), are misplacing their anger, just as feminists in the Muslim world do. Compared to what Muslims would have done in similar circumstances, if Western terrorists had attacked a Muslim country on the scale of 9/11, the American people have shown more heroic self-control, grace, and tolerance than anyone could have expected. This is something that Muslims in the

United States should have noticed—instead of playing a game of defiance with a country in mourning.

Muslims who immigrated to the United States from the Middle East, including Ahmed and myself, all have dual citizenship. If the situation in America was so bad after 9/11 that some felt forced to wear Islamic garb simply to make a point, that act was silly and juvenile. The Islamic attire movement on college campuses cannot be for justice and equality, as is claimed. I think it is done as an expression of defiance against American culture. If the goal of these Muslim women is really equality and justice, then let them demonstrate on behalf of women in Cairo or Mecca, where women cannot legally leave their houses without their husbands' permission.

Wearing Islamic attire on U.S. college campuses is simply an in-your-face way of saying "We support sharia." I once asked a Muslim woman whom I personally know not to be religious at all about her reason for wearing the head cover. Her answer was, "In America, the ethnic look gives one more power and respect." I think she is right. The United States unnecessarily bends over backward to accommodate people who refuse to assimilate into American culture. It is a bad sign that many of us immigrants are getting from the politically correct crowd in the United States; they constantly remind us that they love us just the way we are. Americans who try to protect immigrant cultures, thinking that it is honorable and normal not to assimilate, are actually hurting, rather than helping, immigrant communities. After moving to another country, as I did, most people actually find it very hard *not* to assimilate or learn the new language and way of life. That is why we chose to come to the United States in the first place, to be Americans. But some Americans try to welcome ethnic communities by going overboard in rewarding them for remaining encapsulated in their own culture, language, and pride of their national origin. I think this has produced a few pockets of immigrant groups, even on our college campuses, who use ethnic power to their personal advantage.

I also find it extremely hypocritical when Muslims riot, burn, and kill when an American threatens to burn the Koran, as was the case when a Florida pastor, Terry Jones, said he was going to burn the Koran. The reason this is hypocritical on the part of Muslims is because Muslim governments and individuals habitually confiscate and burn Bibles and other people's holy books. Most Westerners don't realize that the government of Saudi Arabia has engaged in burning Korans—yes, Korans—that belonged to the Shiite minorities in Eastern Saudi Arabia and Bahrain. I received this information about Muslims burning other Muslims' Korans from Bahraini Shiites who were surprised by the audacity of the Sunnis who threatened to kill any American who would dare burn a Koran.

The Koran-burning incident has exposed a one-sided respect for Islam by the U.S. media and politicians that is not reciprocated by Muslims toward Shiite Korans and mosques. The U.S. media failed to do its homework and expose this hypocrisy, and, instead of protecting the right of free speech for Americans, they chose to throw that right to the wolves. The U.S. media have also failed to explain to the Muslim world that Americans as individuals are even protected under the law to burn the U.S. flag, the Bible, and the Koran. I would have liked to see the so-called moderate

Muslims in the United States say they would not go down in history as the reason behind America's suppression of free speech, and if that meant that someone wanted to burn the Koran, then that was his right under the U.S. law that we all enjoy. Unfortunately, no Muslim said that, and the U.S. government and the media caved in. I believe this will not go down well in the history of the United States.

Muslim feminist defenders of sharia have influenced not only U.S. educational institutions but also political institutions in the United States. In 2009, when President Obama spoke to the Muslim world in Cairo, he talked about protecting a woman's right to wear the hijab but never mentioned a woman's right *not* to wear the hijab. Obama's speech was partly written for him by the head-covered White House Muslim adviser Dalia Mogahed, who was born in Egypt. She is an assertive defender of sharia, denies any connection between Islam and terrorism, and defends the Muslim Brotherhood. She is also a firm defender of the Council on American-Islamic Relations (CAIR) and the Islamic Society of North America (ISNA). These organizations have radical ties and are promoters of sharia in the United States. CAIR has been described as an unindicted coconspirator in the terror-finance trial against the Holy Land Foundation and its former officials.

Mogahed's reasoning repeats the same old excuses we Egyptians heard, day in and day out, in defense of Islamic jihad and the oppression of women—she blames others for misunderstanding Islam. Her answers are always given with total confidence and conviction, as she tells her audience that any violent actions by Muslims have nothing to do with Islam. Never mind that Islamic mosques, education, art, and songs all glorify jihad as a holy war for the sake of Allah.

Mogahed brings nothing new to Islamic propaganda, but she certainly sounds assertive, eloquent, and interesting to Americans who are unfamiliar with the same old Islamic propaganda and who find it hard to question a religion. Mogahed has a unique advantage over the classic Islamic sheikh, in that she brings to the United States the traditional views of Islamic sheikhs in a Western-style presentation. Yet in reality, she is not much different from the sheikhs who ridicule those who question Islam with statements such as "Who are you to speak for Islam? Leave the analysis to the experts on Islam." Mogahed's logic is very similar, and, coincidentally, her book *Who Speaks for Islam* is a rejection of critics whom she believes not qualified to speak for Islam. It is a meaningless title. She provides statistics that are designed to confuse the reader in order to show that Muslims are very different and are not all terrorists, which is no news anyway.

Of course, the 1.2 billion Muslims all over the world differ greatly. There is good and bad in every group, but one thing controls all of them, and that is the tyranny of sharia. What Mogahed refuses to admit is that reputable critics of Islam have nothing against the Muslim people, but they correctly deduce that the problem stems from *the ideology of Islam* and its scriptures and commandments. What Mogahed refuses to discuss are the actual laws of sharia, the history of jihad, the ideology and the education that produced 9/11, Islamic imperialism, the denial of human rights, and the oppression of women and minorities. Her answers are usually simplistic, such as the argument that sharia cannot be bad for women because the majority of Muslim women allegedly support sharia.

The bottom line of Mogahed's propaganda and others like her in the United States is the same old complaint that the West does not understand Islam and that with some education and sensitivity training, the West will finally accept Islam as a religion of peace. Her position, as well as that of some other Muslims in our government, has given her a powerful opportunity to enhance the standing of radical Islamist groups in the eyes of the U.S. government. Unfortunately, there is no equal voice given to the reformists and the anti-sharia Muslims or the former Muslims. Yet the responsibility falls on our leaders, who hired and entrusted Muslim Brotherhood figures to work in sensitive positions in our government. Mogahed, who is rumored to be, and I personally believe is, a Muslim Brotherhood member herself, has written speeches for the U.S. president to address the Muslim Brotherhood. I believe this was a glaring conflict of interest that the White House should not have allowed. The end result of the speech was an overwhelming impression on the Arab street that Islamism won and secular reformers were defeated. I will go into more detail on the impact of Barack Obama's Cairo speech in chapter 7.

It may surprise most Americans that the influence of the U.S. women's suffrage movement reached all the way to Turkey and Egypt. The only time that Egypt saw a relatively successful, but mostly cosmetic, feminist movement was in 1919, the year American women acquired the right to vote.

Around the same time, Turkey was also undergoing major reforms instituted by Mustafa Kemal Ataturk and hosted some women conferences, one of which was attended by an Egyptian feminist, Huda Shaarawi (1879–1947). That same year, she led the first women's street demonstration in

Egypt, and later in 1923 she founded the Egyptian Feminist Union, which never had more than 250 members and was composed mostly of wealthy upper- and middle-class women. Shaarawi herself was born into a wealthy family and was married against her will to her cousin, a strong tradition in Egypt at that time. She spent her early years in a harem, an experience she wrote about later in her memoir *Harem Years*. In May 1923, she attended the International Women's Suffrage Alliance in Rome. In a speech at this conference, Shaarawi said that women in ancient Egypt had equal status to men and that only under "foreign domination" had women lost those rights. Shaarawi was correct in saying that it was foreign domination, but she probably was not referring to the Arabian domination that actually diminished the status of women by bringing Islam to Egypt in the seventh century. Sadly, she then used the same argument that all Muslim feminists rely on, when she said that Islam granted women equal rights with men, but that the Koran had been "misinterpreted" by those in power.

On her return from Rome in 1923, Shaarawi did the unthinkable for her time: she took off her veil in the middle of the Cairo train station, declaring the end of the veil. This bold act became the central symbol of her movement.

Because of Shaarawi, my grandmother, my mother, and I have never worn the veil. This courageous woman was not only inspired by a global feminist awareness movement but, more important, was also helped by a more open political climate at the time in Egypt. Islam had become weakened in the early 1920s, particularly because Saudi Arabia was a poor country that could not finance the radicalization of the world around it. Egypt was then a Western-leaning kingdom with some residue of influence from the Ataturk reforms. It had several opposing parties with their own newspapers and a parliament that was not only for show. Sharia law was not in the Egyptian constitution, as it is today. Yet above all, the British and the French had considerable influence in the entire region, and their presence had a positive influence on protecting the human rights of minorities. The Egyptian Muslim Brotherhood was not yet established, and Wahabi Islam, the most radical pure Islam, was limited to and localized inside Saudi Arabia.

Mainly, the 250-member Egyptian feminist movement succeeded in bringing about cosmetic changes, such as giving women freedom not to wear the veil. In the period after World War II, my baby-boom generation of Egyptian middle- and upper-class girls had been encouraged to go to college and later on work. Men and women, however, were still segregated, and dating was never allowed. I am grateful to Hoda Shaarawi because, without her movement, I would never have received the education I did.

Yet Shaarawi probably never could have imagined that her movement, which liberated Egyptian woman from the veil, would be overturned some fifty years later, not by the government but by Egyptian women themselves, who opted to go back to the veil. I remember the growth of Islamist infiltration in Egypt, which started in the seventies after jihadist wars with Israel. Many Egyptians fled the harsh poverty of Egypt to go to countries such as Saudi Arabia and the Arab Gulf states—the same countries that were financing Egypt's wars with Israel. Very quickly, Saudi petro-dollars started to change Egyptian culture and the entire region. This coincided with the powerful radical Islamist movement that swept the

Middle East as a result of the Iranian revolution. Saudi Arabia radicalized Sunni Muslim countries, and Iran radicalized the Shiites, and both groups ended up feeding on each other.

At that time, just like my mother and my siblings, not all of the women in Egypt wanted to wear the veil, and a small number refuse to do so even today. Yet the copycat tendency spread quickly, and many women who had initially rejected the veil were left in a quagmire: whether to be perceived as devout Muslims or as outcast rebel apostates. The majority chose the former, because perception is everything in Muslim society.

How can feminism be practiced openly, let alone survive under such conditions? Again and again in the Middle East, the passage of time has not necessarily led to progress, liberty, and positive results. Throughout the history of Islam, there have been cycles of reform and attempts to change society that ended with no gains being made. Muslim feminists have never succeeded in achieving serious reforms, such as the abolition of polygamy, equal inheritance rights, or the right to marry whomever they wish. These are all demands that go against sharia, and, as I mentioned earlier, women who make these demands are called apostates. To muzzle Muslim feminists, the Arab media will usually accuse them of borrowing corrupt and subversive ideas from foreign infidel Zionists and enemies of Islam.

Other than a few Iranian feminist organizations operating from the West and protesting honor killings and the abuse of women in Iran, there is no strong grassroots Islamic feminist movement in the Middle East. Islamic feminists, both in the Middle East and in the West, who still call themselves Muslims have no choice but to continue supporting the illusion that Islam was originally respectful of women and only later became corrupted against women.

With every serious attempt to reform women's lives, there is the opposing harsh reality of sharia: doors that are shut and windows closed to keep women in the confines of the Islamic jail. As soon as women work around one law that was designed to control them, another one pops up that is even harsher. The Muslim feminist movement cannot function successfully under such a hostile environment. Islamic sharia is the gun pointed at their heads.

To sum up, Islamic feminism is a twisted kind of feminism that champions pride in Islamic bondage. This is all that Muslim women are allowed to do. Islamic feminism features a unique kind of aggressive submission to the abusive laws of Islam—a kind of a mass Stockholm syndrome where the victim, the Muslim woman, identifies with and defends the oppressor, the Islamic establishment and its laws. As a result, in the Middle East there are many assertive militant Muslim women who act in the role of "virtue police" to oppress other women. This self-destructive form of feminism pits one woman against another in a competition to defend the religion that taught her to loathe herself and that makes her loathe other women as well.

Activist Muslim women in the West invest their energy in promoting the building of a mosque at Ground Zero in New York City or changing America's views of Islam, but they are nowhere to be found when there are reports of honor killing, the oppression of women, the flogging and stoning of women, female genital mutilation, polygamy, and the killing of apostates and blasphemers, all of which are being perpetrated today in the name of Islam. Far too many Muslim women in the West close their eyes to the plight of their sisters in the Muslim world, who suffer quietly in an often-unforgiving culture.

Where are the wealthy Saudi women who could be helping their sisters in distress in Darfur? Where is the Muslim Mother Teresa in Iraq, Egypt, or Afghanistan? Where is the compassion of Muslim women who could be defending other oppressed and wronged women? Has sharia deadened their hearts, closed their eyes, and dulled their senses?

The intellectual cowardice of some women who advocate sharia in the United States and Europe is staggering. While the few feminists in the Middle East are being humiliated, silenced, threatened, or killed, many of their sisters in the West simply ignore them. They do not want to expose anything negative about Islam, and if that means not supporting women in the Middle East, then so be it. That is why when the oppressed women of Afghanistan were imprisoned in their homes and deprived of an education or a job, none of these atrocities were uncovered or reported by Muslim women or groups. These are the same groups that today are demonstrating on college campuses with their burkas against the so-called discrimination in the United States. America needs to know that these women have no case and zero credibility.

Some female members of Muslim student associations on U.S. college campuses attack me and other speakers who criticize sharia. In one instance, an unnamed Muslim student at George Washington University, whose accent sounded Egyptian, yelled at a protest, "I want the sharia law imposed in my country."[4] Note her choice of the word *imposed*. I presume that she meant "the United States" when she said "my country," because sharia is already imposed in Muslim countries, on one level or another. Again, these holier-than-thou women are practicing the only feminism allowed to them in Islam: pride in bondage.

Liberty and equality for women in the Middle East are closely linked to defeating sharia. By people discrediting sharia, men will also be liberated from their obligation to do violent jihad, which may perhaps lead to the elimination of Islamic terrorism against the non-Muslim world.

It is not only in the best interests of Muslims to discredit and defeat sharia; it is also in the best interests of Western democracies. The West is extremely vulnerable to Islamism and sharia supporters who have risen to influential positions in the West, as we will see in the next chapter.

7

Western Vulnerability

The Arab Spring fooled and confused many in the West, even some seasoned observers, who enthusiastically believed that with the removal of dictatorships, life would get better for everyone in the Middle East. Some even compared the Arab Spring to the fall of the Berlin Wall and the collapse of the Soviet Union. Yet Islamic concepts, such as "freedom from oppression," are very different from those concepts in the West. To many Muslims, achieving freedom from oppression means life in the ideal Islamic state under Allah's law. Sadly, the world is gradually realizing that the 2011 Islamic revolutions followed in the same footsteps as previous Islamic revolutions, which brought only superficial changes but then fell back into the same mold of Islamic sharia.

In the post-9/11 world, the amount of information being tossed around about the ideology of Islam has been staggering. By now, people in the West should fully understand the dynamics of revolutions in the Middle East, let alone Islamic culture and the danger that Islam presents to the free world. Why do so many of them not comprehend these issues?

As I described in previous chapters, many influential Western politicians, academics, and the mainstream media have ignored or altogether rejected the basic facts about Islam. Despite the brutal orchestrated beheadings, stonings, honor killings, torture, and hanging of innocent men and women in the name of Islam by those who tell the world they are the true Muslims, it has become taboo in the United States to show fear or be alarmed at both the stealthy and the violent forms of Islamic jihad.

Even when Islamists in the United Kingdom declared that the three towns of Dewsbury, Radford, and Tower Hamlets were independent Islamic "emirates" and would operate entirely outside British law and be ruled by sharia, little concern was expressed by the Western media or UK politicians, who are civil servants sworn to uphold their constitution. Where is the outrage in Great Britain? Western citizens' legitimate concern about, and fear of, the Islamic threat to their way of life is often dismissed by elected civil servants and is suppressed by the media as being racism.

Criminalizing the criticism of Islam is prevalent in Europe today, yet this goes against the basic freedom and welfare of European citizens. Such repression and shaming of Europeans and Americans who reject the influence of sharia on their governments and societies will only exacerbate matters and increase tension between them and Muslim immigrants. This problem could be alleviated by passing simple legislation that would clearly make sharia and other foreign laws that violate human rights and the

U.S. constitution illegal. Instead, Western governments have chosen to consider sharia and even defend it, in the case of the United Kingdom. By enforcing one-sided respect toward the culture of Islam in Europe and the United States and placing the pressure of absorbing change entirely on the shoulders of Western citizens, Western governments and media are setting the stage for a disaster.

Such a disaster actually did happen in Norway on July 25 when a deranged Norwegian terrorist, Anders Behring Breivik, took matters into his own hands and went on a shooting rampage, killing more than seventy-six people, mostly teenagers. Such acts of terror were unheard of in Norway before the impact of Islam on that nation, and the violence left many stunned. Could this be the beginning of civil unrest in Europe, in response to the constant threat of Islamic terror all over that continent? Only time will tell.

There is not enough discussion in the West on the psychological traumas of 9/11, the Fort Hood massacre, the London and Madrid bombings, and all of the Islamic terror plots around the world. The United States must recognize the effect of such trauma on the American people and even on the U.S. military, whose freedom of speech regarding Islam has been muzzled. So far, the twenty-first century has been the century of Islamic terror and unrest, which are negatively rocking the world both psychologically and financially, in the form of a high price tag to fund national security.

Hardly a day goes by when an Islamic leader does not express his wish to destroy the United States, the United Kingdom, Israel, and all non-Muslim countries. There is no doubt that such Islamic threats, both verbal and in the form of terrorist acts and defiance of Western lifestyles, negatively affect the psyches of Westerners, whether they know it or not. Muslims around the world should understand this and be more sympathetic of it; they should stand against the Islamists who issue the threats. The reckless daily barrage of Islamic threats all around the world will not prompt Westerners to love Muslims because, unfortunately, that is human nature. Islamists have produced fear and trauma in the Western mind, and these feelings are now directed against Islam.

Because my first language is Arabic—and because I watch Arab TV, read Arab newspapers, and understand what Islamists are saying—I am more afraid than the average American is. Some U.S. and Muslim groups treat me and others like me without mercy for daring to lay bare the truth. Yet my fear is not an unreasonable phobia, despite those cruel accusers calling us critics Islamophobes. Why have statements such as the following not aired on American TV to expose who is inciting the Muslim world and to show that terrorists are not fringe groups rejected by mainstream Islam? Why are we hiding the truth from the American people, and why am I often told that my fear of statements such as this is unreasonable?

> Four pounds of anthrax—in a suitcase this big—carried by a fighter through tunnels from Mexico into the U.S., are guaranteed to kill 330,000 Americans within a single hour, if it is properly spread in population centers there. What would be a horrific terror attack that will make 9/11 appear as child play in comparison. Am I right? There is no need for airplanes, conspiracies, timings, and so on. One person,

with the courage to carry four pounds of anthrax, will go to the White House lawn, and will spread this "confetti" all over them, and then will do these cries of joy. It will turn into a real "celebration."[1]

These words were not uttered in the secret caves of al Qaeda, but on Al-Jazeera TV by a Kuwaiti professor, Abdullah Al-Nafisi.

The terror card is not kept a secret. Many Muslim sheikhs proudly state that whenever there is a demand for a few jihadis to die for Allah, a thousand volunteer. Yet Western culture has made it taboo to take them at their word, even after 9/11. The U.S. media never report a newsworthy story such as the one I cited here. The media in the United States often practice self-censorship when it comes to Islam and go out of their way to omit coverage of stories broadcast over Arab media, which I watch every day. In that sense, Western media, which provide a window to the world on how Americans think, have abided by the sharia law never to criticize Islam or Muslims, even as Islamist threats hang over the West, waiting to explode at any time in the form of a terrorist act. The victims here are the American public, who are not treated as adults and who deserve to learn the truth about the enemy we are supposedly fighting. The trauma that many Americans have suffered in the aftermath of 9/11 is not being acknowledged as real and worthy of respect by a media telling Americans that the enemy is not really an enemy.

It is a mystery why some of the most intelligent people in the United States treat Islam this way. Why do they often go out of their way to embrace Islam and even promote certain shady Muslim groups and characters? No matter what plots are uncovered, how many public beheadings are shown on Al-Jazeera Arab TV, how many victims are terrorized, how many women are victims of honor killings, and how many threats are made, America remains split, with many continuing to disregard the uneasy truth about Islam.

Some believe that this is happening out of fear, but I think it is much more than fear, because those who deny the truth about Islam are not merely silent; they actually defend the indefensible. I have finally come to terms with what I believe is the truth: some Americans, including many on the left, simply admire and respect an ideology that is so contrary to the conventional wisdom in the West: Islamic pride in supremacy, control and power (even reckless power), petro-dollars, its disregard of Western taboos, the in-your-face male chauvinism, female pride in subservience, the eagerness to win at any cost, and the nostalgia of having a cause to die for. This is more than simply a Stockholm syndrome infecting certain Americans; it has become actual admiration of one's enemy.

The pro-Islam crowd in the United States does not stop at misinformation, self-censorship, or failing to report news from the Middle East, but they also engage in vicious attacks to silence those, myself included, who expose the Islamist agenda. They have little regard for our First Amendment rights, and they use the tactics of shaming and name calling—deriding us as Islamophobes, racists, bigots, and polarizing figures. Anyone with an opinion can be called a polarizing figure, but that expression is never used to describe those who, for instance, burn the American flag or produce a movie about the assassination of President George W. Bush while he is in office. Name calling is reserved for those who have a different opinion from antiestablishment Americans and their supporters in the media. As for the word *Islamophobe*, it has become meaningless, because I and all of the others who speak out are truly afraid for America's future in regard to Islam, and rightfully so. No illusions about that.

Something is wrong with this picture. It is the beginning of a slippery slope into tyranny, a picture I am very familiar with. Having lived under tyranny, I recognize its early signs. The conventional wisdom in the West is that we should be more concerned with not offending peace-loving Muslims and thus should suppress the truth, rather than face the reality about Islam. The fact that not all Muslims are terrorists has become a good reason to avoid reporting on Islamic tyranny or making a big deal out of it. This is equivalent to not reporting on the horrors of Nazi Germany or Japanese assaults on the United States during World War II lest we offend German or Japanese Americans. I have never seen the West be so cowardly about an issue, even when it is as extreme as the Islamic racism and slavery that are prevalent today in Arab Islamic Sudan against black Christian southern Sudan. The topic is hardly ever reported on, even by black Americans.

Wherever Islam goes, a Stockholm syndrome seems to afflict the people touched by its terror and tyranny. Just like the anthrax confetti the Arab professor recommended to poison the minds of Americans, there was mass damage inflicted on Americans as a result of 9/11 and the many smaller terror attacks that followed. We must never underestimate the impact of terror on a mass scale. Stockholm syndrome is a proven condition that results in an emotional attachment, an identification, or a bond between victim and victimizer. The mere fact that the captor spared one's life can prompt a feeling of gratitude, even admiration, for the captor, who is then seen as a savior. When the terror occurs on a large scale, it can produce a mass Stockholm syndrome, even toward a specific culture.

Psychologist William E. Schlenger said that the 9/11 attacks "represent an unprecedented exposure to trauma within the borders of the United States. Today, people from sea to shining sea are still dealing with the emotional repercussions of the events of September 11, 2001."[2] Yael Danieli, a New York City clinical psychologist and a founding director of the International Society for Traumatic Stress Studies, said, "September 11 was a terrible loss—not just in terms of lost life, but in terms of a lost way of life."[3]

Remember the expression "America held hostage" that was often heard on U.S. TV during the 1979 American hostage crisis in Iran? Now the American mind is being held hostage by Islamism. Many Americans now identify with their terrorist oppressors. Could it be a mere coincidence that the American people have voted in, not only its first black president, but a president whose name rhymes with Osama? The question is not meant to be an insult to President Barack Obama, but a legitimate questioning of the psychological motivations of the American people after 9/11, their sharp divisions and fears. That is what terrorism does to a nation; it splits it apart and throws it into disarray.

The whole world looked up to the United States as a symbol of protection and power from the evils of the world, yet the perception in the Middle East is that America is a paper tiger, that America is afraid to even name its true enemy or condemn the countries that produced the 9/11 terrorists. Somehow, we gave a pass to the Saudi and Egyptian cultures of hate. America's reaction to 9/11 up until today has not been strong enough, and I do not mean only military action.

September 11 put Americans in a weaker position, filled them with self-blame, and engendered a more forgiving attitude toward Islam, but it has given Muslims a sense of empowerment. Muslim American leaders, such as the chairman of the Council on American Islamic Relations (CAIR), Nihad Awad, told the Saudi newspaper *Ukaz* that "34,000 Americans have converted to Islam following the events of September 11, and this is the highest rate reached in the U.S. since Islam arrived there." I am not sure how accurate Awad's figures are, because one-third of converts to Islam in the United States convert out of it within two years. Immediately after 9/11, Sheikh Raid Sallah, the head of the Islamic movement in Israel, also told a rally, "Oh, peoples of the West . . . we say to you: We are the masters of the world and we are the repository of all good [in the world], because we are 'the best people, delivered for mankind' [Koran, 3:111]. We do not hesitate, Oh Bush and Blair; we invite you to Islam, enter Islam, you and your peoples."[4]

Terror can play tricks on the minds of some of the most intelligent individuals, and it has caused some people to convert to the ideology that killed three thousand of their fellow U.S. citizens. The serious Islamic threat to Western civilization has been reduced to endless shouting matches, pro and con, as if the threat were nothing more than a discussion about the flavor of the month. The U.S. jury has not yet come back with a verdict on the nature of the ideology that is behind 9/11. It is all a matter of opinion, and never mind the facts. As I described in an earlier chapter, every poll taken in the Middle East on the death of bin Laden showed that a large majority of Muslims were saddened and angered by his death and many have threatened revenge, yet again on the United States. Strong indications show that the government and the intelligence agencies of Pakistan were helping bin Laden hide. The conspiracy to hide bin Laden could have been much larger than the Pakistani government and may have included many other Islamic governments, such as Saudi Arabia. For the United States to continue telling the American people that the problem was only al Qaeda is simply untrue. The U.S. citizen has been deceived.

On March 17, 2011, I wrote an article titled "Former Muslims Excluded from King Hearings," in which I expressed my disappointment that former Muslims were not represented in U.S. congressman Peter King's hearing, "Extent of Radicalization in the American Muslim Community and That Community's Response." A long list of people testified on both sides of the issue; many of them were Muslims who took opposing points of view.

Former Muslims could have illuminated a side of radical Islam in the United States that is a threat to our national security and that none of the guests at the hearing were able—or willing—to discuss. We former Muslims all share similar personal experiences of why we left Islam and why we moved to the United States. We had similar reactions to what went on in the mosques that drove us to leave and never return. We made similar choices: either to continue supporting Islam or to love America and its Constitution. We have similar knowledge of how certain terror groups, such as Hamas and the Muslim Brotherhood, are openly supported as legitimate and how excuses are given for bin Laden's terrorist acts. We were given similar advice on how not to assimilate in America and how to make Islam the law of the land. Finally, we came to similar conclusions about how mosques advocate sharia, anti-Semitism, jihad, and an "us against them" mentality in order to reject American values.

Muslim groups and the mainstream media rose up in arms against the King hearings, claiming that they were biased against one group, Muslims, and thereby violated the civil rights of Muslims. The Muslim groups that claim they are victims of the bigoted King hearings are the same groups that refused to sign the pledge that Former Muslims United repeatedly sent to them, seeking their support against the sharia commandment to execute apostates. They are also the same Islamic groups that attacked Rifqa Bary, the seventeen-year-old girl who, when she escaped from her family, was threatened for leaving Islam. Muslim groups supported her parents, spread hateful rumors about the girl, and provided the family with legal help to fight the girl in court.

It is preposterous for Muslim groups to deny, as they do, that there are good reasons for holding hearings on radical Islam and to claim that their civil rights are being violated. Their claims cannot pass the "laugh test" when they are the ones who violate the religious freedom of former Muslims. Pressure from Islamic groups is probably the reason the King hearings did not include any former Muslims.

In another instance, former Muslims were not excluded from a government hearing. On April 8, 2011, I was pleased to participate in a set of hearings on homeland security in the New York State Senate. In response to a question by Chairman Greg Ball (R-Putnam), I described how, as a youngster, I and other Muslim children were indoctrinated into hatred of the West, specifically the United States and Israel, and into jihad and martyrdom. Suddenly, I was interrupted by state senator Eric Adams (D-Brooklyn), who held up a copy of the Koran and asked me with contempt, "Are you saying that this book teaches hate?" Then he looked at the chairman and said, "This is offending this hearing by having her here." Adams declared, "This is not our enemy. . . . You're bringing hate, hate and poison, into a diverse country." The chairman then instructed Adams to pipe down and suggested that he was playing to the TV cameras. I was able to squeeze in some words to Senator Adams, telling him that the book he was defending allows slavery, sexual slavery, the beating of women, and violent jihad. I am not sure whether he heard me or even cared to know.

Unfortunately, Thomas Kaplan, in an article in the *New York Times*, described the hearings as a debate on whether "Muslims are predisposed to terrorism."[5] That is not accurate. Kaplan added that I and another speaker have "advanced" that claim, the other speaker being Frank Gaffney, the president of the Center for Security Policy. Yet he was not able to quote me saying anything even close to an assertion that Muslims are predisposed to terrorism. That was never the topic of the debate, I was never asked that question, and I never said anything to insinuate this. I have always believed that Muslims are the primary victims of sharia, and I have a lot of sympathy toward the oppressed peoples of the Middle East. My degree is in sociology and anthropology, and it is inconceivable that I would make as reckless a comment as Mr. Kaplan claimed. My criticism is always aimed at the ideology of political and legal Islam and not at the people. I always emphasize that there are good and bad people in every religion, but that I have the right to speak against a religion that condemns me and many others to death.

Kaplan concluded the article with a claim that the technical part of the discussion on terror in New York City subways and airports was boring, as witnessed by the fact that at least three people in the audience were asleep. Even though it is common for a few people to fall asleep in most long hearings and conferences, the mainstream media take notice only when it happens during an event they describe negatively. This article reflects the views of many in the mainstream media who ridicule serious discussions about protecting ourselves from Islamic terrorism and, worse, call them an attack on all Muslims. All of which should end the conversation.

I am, of course, aware of the enormity and complexity of the Islamic threat and how the West must play some games as well and handle such explosive topics very carefully. Yet the West does not have to go out of its way to sound apologetic to Muslims or to embrace and befriend the Muslim Brotherhood, a terrorist organization that is losing credibility among the reformists who sparked the revolution in Egypt. The Brotherhood has always been a destabilizing factor that caused coups, assassinations, and assassination attempts in every administration in Egypt since its establishment eighty years ago. The Brotherhood has given birth to or inspired many other Islamist groups across the Middle East, including al Qaeda itself.

With today's alternative media, the United States has the ability to reach the Arab street and convince Arabs of its position. By telling the truth about the threat of radical Islam, America should have nothing to fear if it defines its enemy properly and understands that it is much more than al Qaeda—that the enemy is legal Islam embodied in oppressive sharia, political Islam bent on establishing a one-party Islamic state, and the institution of violent jihad that uses terrorism as a solution. These are all legitimate threats to our way of life, and we should never shy away from clearly articulating them. The truth is that these threats are also threats to Muslim reformers, and the issues are the very ones that many Muslim countries are struggling with. These threats make up the same enemy the pro-democracy advocates who started the Arab Spring were rebelling against, but the Islamists are now twisting their arms. How can the United States say it is on the side of reformers but act as if it is on the side of the Muslim Brotherhood? Where is America's credibility?

If the United States openly puts forth its objections and asserts its unequivocal right to protect its way of life, it will be more respected in the Arab world, and this will also empower the reformists. Such a unified stand by Americans would be much more powerful than attacking terrorists in their holes in Afghanistan. The United States should never be worried about being viewed as anti-Islam if it clearly defines its position. Muslims should understand and perhaps even identify with America's deep concerns, because Muslims can see that all religions, whether it be Buddhism, Hinduism, or the many sects of Judaism and Christianity, live in peace in America. Why should the U.S. government, with all of the problems it faces, pick on Islam alone, especially when many Muslim countries have the oil that the

West needs? America did not declare war on Islam; radical Islam and its secret supporters declared war on America, and Muslims know it. The game that radical Islam plays is an old trick—crying the loudest, claiming to be a victim, so that no one can figure out its true objectives.

Islam's critics, myself included, will not be deterred by name calling and will always assert our First Amendment rights. We will not fall into the Stockholm syndrome trap. Our goal is not to criticize any religion capriciously, especially a religion such as Islam, which prides itself on taking vengeance with its sword. Our goal is to expose an evil ideology. If a religion expands to become a totalitarian state that gives itself the right to commit violence against others, then it would be insane to stay silent. Tyranny should never be a religious right, and that is why all freedom-loving people must speak out. Unlike the appeasers, we are stronger on the basis of our moral values.

Yet the United States and Western culture have been caught unprepared by the Islamic agenda at a vulnerable stage in Western history, just as the Byzantine and Persian empires were in the seventh century. Hopefully, ours will be a better ending. To facilitate this, specific political and cultural vulnerabilities in the West vis-à-vis Islam must be addressed.

The first vulnerability the West faces is political. Islam does not believe it can survive without sharia, and obedience to sharia cannot be achieved without government enforcement. Thus, government is everything to Islam; it is the ultimate method of preserving Islam. That is the main reason Islam always aims to penetrate the governments of every country where Muslims live. Government to Islam is like water to fish and air to humans. Anyone who watches and listens to Islamic preaching will quickly realize this fact. The bottom line and the ultimate goal of Muslim groups in the United States are to penetrate the U.S. government. That is how the groups' success is measured by the people who finance and support them. When the first Muslim congressman, Keith Ellison, was elected, cries of "Allahu Akbar" (the call of Islamic triumph) were heard in the audience.

This is not an isolated instance. There is a Muslim group that gathers annually in Washington, D.C., to pray over the anniversary of the death of Ayatollah Khomeini, an open enemy of the United States and a sharia advocate. A young Muslim woman at a recent event said, "Not only did he start, you know, the Islamic revolution in Iran, but . . . all Muslims now. . . celebrate the revolution of Iran as an Islamic uprising."[6] In her broken English, what this woman meant was that the Arab Spring was in fact an Islamic revolution following the example of Iran. The Muslims in these gatherings are U.S. citizens who would like to see sharia replace the U.S. Constitution.

The U.S. government has adopted a policy of outreach to the Muslim community, especially after 9/11. What the United States considers outreach, however, the Islamists consider an opportunity. At our invitation, Islam has made itself very comfortable inserting itself into U.S. politics. President Obama in particular has bent over backward to eliminate the words *terrorism*, *jihad*, or *Islam* in reference to what is clearly Islamic terrorism and has hired devout Muslims to assist him in his outreach to Muslims both inside and outside the United States.

In addition, in 2009 President Obama gave legitimacy to the sharia lovers when he chose to speak at the campus of the Islamic Al Azhar University in Cairo, the guardian of sharia, to address the so-called Muslim World. His audience was composed largely of members of the Muslim Brotherhood and/or their supporters, while the president of Egypt, whom the Muslim Brotherhood had attempted to assassinate, was not in attendance. From my perspective, the speech was one of appeasement to the culture that produced Mohammed Attah, the leader of the 9/11 terrorists.

If the purpose of the Obama speech was to make Muslims love Obama, it certainly has accomplished its goal. Yet in attaining that goal, Obama allowed several inaccuracies into his speech, such as this one: "Islam has always been a part of America's story," and "throughout history, Islam has demonstrated through words and deeds the possibilities of religious tolerance and racial equality." He also made the following exaggerations: "Since our founding, American Muslims have enriched the United States. They have fought in our wars, they have served in our government, they have stood for civil rights, they have started businesses, they have taught at our universities, they've excelled in our sports arenas, they've won Nobel Prizes, built our tallest building, and lit the Olympic Torch."[7] These are the kind of exaggerations and inaccuracies that Muslims live for. To justify jihad in America, some Muslims actually say that the word *California* originates from the word *Califate* and that Christopher Columbus could not have discovered America without Muslim help. Muslims are desperate to justify their eagerness to conquer America, and Obama's appeasement gratified jihadists' aspirations. These comments were written for Obama by his Islamic adviser at the time, Dalia Mogahed, the devout, Egyptian-born, head-covered Muslim, who is also a Muslim Brotherhood and Hamas sympathizer.

Obama said, "I consider it part of my responsibility as president of the United States to fight against negative stereotypes of Islam wherever they appear."[8] Obama failed to take the opportunity to remind Muslims that freedom is a basic right in the United States, and that it is not the responsibility of Western governments to silence criticism of any religion, ideology, or person of power, even criticism of the president of the United States himself. As a consequence, many Egyptians believe that criticism of Islam in America will be made illegal or will be patrolled by the U.S. government.

Obama also left an impression that the reason Jews are in Israel is because of their persecution in Europe. He said, "The Jewish homeland is rooted in a tragic history that cannot be denied." That plays into the hands of many Muslims, who believe that the only reason Jews came to Israel was because they were chased out of Europe.

In his Cairo speech, Obama also defended Muslims' right to pay *zakat* alms when he said, "I'm committed to working with American Muslims to ensure that they can fulfill *zakat*." Obama's advisers failed to tell him that sharia dictates that about 20 percent of zakat must go to the jihadist fighters, and that is why much of the funds that Islamist groups in the United States collected for the purpose of zakat have gone to organizations such as Hamas and Hezbollah. That statement left an impression on Muslims that the U.S. president was more concerned with appeasement than accuracy.

Obama also consistently used the words "holy Koran," instead of simply "the Koran," an expression that is not used by ordinary Muslims, except for Islamists who also consistently say, "Peace be upon him," whenever the name Mohammed is mentioned. It is important to understand how President Obama's speech led many Muslims to believe certain misconceptions, such as the implication that U.S. law will not allow criticism of Islam and that America's policy of supporting Israel has weakened.

With his Cairo speech and other actions of Islamic appeasement, President Obama has set a new standard that future U.S. presidents might find difficult to follow. The next U.S. administration might find it hard to please the Muslim world after several of the pro-Islamic policies Obama has set. For instance, how will a future U.S. president be viewed by the Muslim world if he does not bow to the Saudi king, as Obama did? If the future president has a policy not to treat Muslims with kid gloves and begins to treat Muslim leaders like adults, will he or she be criticized as being hostile to Islam? If the next administration goes back to naming the threat *Islamic terrorism*, will the president be called Hitler by the media? Are we going to cheer when Islamists throw their shoes at our future U.S. president simply for not supporting radical Islam? Will Western media call conservative U.S. leaders who want to protect America racists and bigots for not accepting the Muslim Brotherhood as Obama has done? In view of what Obama is doing today, that is something to think about.

Another example of such appeasement is the deputy chief of staff to Secretary of State Hillary Clinton, Huma Abedin, a practicing Muslim and the wife of former congressman Anthony Weiner, who is Jewish. Under Islamic law, it is a sinful act of apostasy for a Muslim woman to marry a non-Muslim unless he converts to Islam, but Abedin has never been criticized for her marriage to a Jew by any Muslim entity, either in the United States or in Saudi Arabia, where her mother lives and works. This is very unusual, and perhaps she was given a pass and was forgiven by Muslim leaders for what is considered by Islam a major sin, because Arabs believe she is their person at the U.S. State Department.

Walid Shoebat, the author of *God's War on Terror*, has reported that Huma's mother, Saleha Mahmood Abedin, was named by Al-Jazeera and major Arab newspapers to be on a list of members of the Muslim Sisterhood, the female affiliate of the Muslim Brotherhood. Shoebat also reported that Huma's brother, Hassan Abedin, is a fellow at the Oxford Centre for Islamic Studies (OCIS), and that he partners with a number of Muslim Brotherhood members on the board, including al Qaeda associate Omar Naseef and the notorious Muslim Brotherhood leader Sheikh Youssef Qaradawi; both have been listed as OCIS trustees. Naseef continues to serve as board chairman. Shoebat's article does not imply that Huma's brother has done anything wrong, but that he is active in the Islamic community in the United Kingdom. That being the case, it is hard to imagine why Muslims, who are very vocal about Muslim women when they sin, are suddenly silent about Huma's marriage to a highly visible Jewish man.[9]

The U.S. government has also allowed several shady Islamist characters to visit or move to the United States. The State Department has recently lifted the ban on Tariq Ramadan entering the country. Ramadan is the grandson of the founder of the Muslim Brotherhood, Hasan Al Banna, and has ties to several Islamist groups. The powerful Turkish imam Fethullah Gulen was also able to enter the United States after escaping from Turkey, where he was indicted in 2000 for attempting to overthrow the secular Turkish government. Gulen believes in "the new world Islamic Order." In one of his sermons, he said, "The philosophy of our service is that we open a house somewhere and, with the patience of a spider, we lay our web to wait for people to get caught in the web; and we teach those who do."[10] Gulen was also quoted in another sermon as saying, "You must move in the arteries of the system without anyone noticing your existence until you reach all the power centers.... You must wait for the time when you are complete and conditions are ripe, until we can shoulder the entire world and carry it."[11]

While the U.S. government is busy doing "outreach" to, or appeasement of, the Muslim world that continues to terrorize us, it has neglected and ignored the feelings of many Americans, the victims of terror and the people whom government officials were elected to serve. The West's political vulnerability is compounded by its dependence on Middle Eastern oil and the petro-dollars in the hands of Islamic groups all over the United States, who use and abuse every opportunity called "outreach" that results from American naiveté.

This is probably the first time in U.S. history when there are clear indications that the U.S. government and media are mistreating the American people in favor of a foreign entity. American officials, on one hand, support the building of a mosque near Ground Zero, despite the fact that it is contrary to what most Americans want, while, on the other hand, they denounce the use of the expression "Islamic terrorism" because it will hurt the feelings of Muslims. Clearly, this can be perceived as discrimination against the majority of Americans.

President Obama and New York City mayor Michael Bloomberg have humiliated and failed to appreciate the genuine feelings of many Americans. Some family members expressed their concern that calls for prayers, "Allahu Akbar," will be heard from Ground Zero, which is the same cry the terrorists gave before slamming the airplanes into the Twin Towers. Imam Feisal Abdul Rauf shamelessly called the mosque project "Cordoba" house, after the Islamic triumph in the Spanish city of Cordoba. Rauf and his ilk really think we are too stupid to figure out that he chose the word *Cordoba* to signify the triumph of Islamic jihad. He is an Islamist in sheep's clothing, calling himself "a man of peace" and grandiosely comparing himself to Mahatma Gandhi or President Anwar Sadat. It's a hollow expression, though, because we are all for peace. Rauf's deceit and double-talk were clear when his book was published in Malaysia with the title *A Call to Prayer from the World Trade Center Rubble: Islamic Dawa [Proselytizing] in the Heart of America Post 9/11*, while the same book was published in English under the title *What's Right with Islam Is What's Right with America.*

The sharia commandment for Muslims to lie, exaggerate, and slander has become second nature for Islamists such as Rauf. He and his wife and his supporters believe they can easily pull the rug out from under the feet of Americans, whom they think are too stupid to figure out who he really is.

The second vulnerability to Islam that the West faces is cultural. What void does Islam fill in the West? Why are some Western women and men embracing Islam?

When I first moved to the United States more than thirty years ago, two families on my street consisted of grandparents bringing up their grandchildren. This was quite unusual to me, and I was very curious to learn whether the parents were dead or disabled. When I discovered that the parents had been found to be unfit by the state, I was astounded. I had assumed that drug and alcohol addiction in the United States—the cause cited for these parents' unfitness—was mostly a juvenile problem, but to my surprise, it is widespread among adults, parents, and even grandparents. This reality in American society has produced many needy and vulnerable young people, a prime target group for Islamic proselytizing.

People with alcohol and drug dependencies gravitate to controlling ideologies and systems of government that do not require much personal choice and responsibility. They seek a totalitarian authority that gives them benefits simply for keeping out of the government's way and for being obedient citizens, as long as they do not rock the boat. This kind of government is found in totalitarian socialist and Islamic countries that seek zombies and not alert citizens. Islam fits the needs of such vulnerable people.

Some Western women feel alienated by the antimale feminist movement's promise they can have it all and don't need a man. In contrast, the Muslim man, dark and handsome, appeals to them like the prince on the white horse whom every young girl dreams of. He tells her he wants marriage, commitment, and for her to stay home and take care of the kids, while he works and handles the finances. Many segments of Western society have neglected women's hunger for a traditional family, and the promises of Muslim men suddenly sound very appealing to women who have a yearning for marriage and motherhood.

I have received many e-mails from American and European women who converted to Islam following a love affair with a Muslim man, only to fall out of love a couple of years later after they had a couple of kids. The story keeps repeating itself, but the lesson we must learn from this is that America needs to nurture the natural tendencies of male and female and give more respect to the traditional family. The right to have an untraditional lifestyle does not have to clash with the desires of many women. America must find the right balance between these conflicting views about lifestyle choices without intimidating or insulting anyone.

Although respect for Islam has been increasing in the United States, respect for Christianity and Judaism has been decreasing. American schools are inviting Muslim sheikhs and shady figures to teach Islam in high schools and colleges, while preventing Christian leaders from doing the same. Islam is taking full advantage of this multicultural vulnerability the United States has trapped itself in. We are creating a new generation of Americans who will have no respect for the culture, the religions, and the values that made America great, the country that many people cross oceans simply to live in. Americans should see the long lines of Muslims who are dying to move to the United States or any other Western country that will take them, to flee the tyranny of Islam.

Today's American culture has also been unfair to men. Just look at all of the silly commercials on TV ridiculing the role of the man in the family, as they show a smart, thin, sexy wife with her fat, sloppy husband. To fix a fault, America tends to go to the opposite extreme, instead of finding a happy medium. In the case of the man, America has rejected his masculinity, ridiculed him, feminized him, and even abused him—all for the purpose of counteracting centuries of discrimination against women.

Such an atmosphere produces vulnerable young American men who are looking for support for their male identity, and those are the people whom Islamists seek out. Islamic culture provides many channels for male friendship and bonding in fields beyond just sports. What appeals to Western men is that Islam tells them it is fine and even more advantageous to be male.

To avoid being sucked into the stagnant and oppressive culture of Islam, America must end its destructive fighting with itself. The ultimate solution for the United States is to find the right equilibrium to bring together the traditional and the untraditional, the religious and the nonreligious, to pick the good values out of the old and the new, and never to prop up one group in order to punish another. That is the only way to create harmony in a society—by elevating everyone.

There is nobility in cultures like that of the United States that promote respect for other cultures and strive to be fair to all minorities. No country in the world has accomplished that more than America has. Yet unfortunately, some influential segments of U.S. society take this to the extreme, at the expense of other vital segments of society. Multiculturalists want to see the United States as a bigger reflection of the United Nations building or the television series *Star Trek*, believing we can all live in perfect peace and harmony, while keeping our colorful, different exteriors, clothes, habits, and food. They believe we can always identify ourselves as members of a certain group, religion, or race, while rejecting assimilation into a common culture. That is exactly how America should be in their eyes. Otherwise, they believe it is racist and bigoted if it caters to the natural tendency of any culture to gravitate toward the comfort zone of a coherent homogeneous entity.

Yet the standard that multiculturalists set for the less-developed world is different. Less-developed nations get a pass. These cultures can be as ethnocentric, proud, nationalistic, and supremacist as they want. Multiculturalists have allowed themselves a paternalistic controlling position toward ethnically unique cultures. Just like their concern for whales, they feel that less-developed cultures must be preserved from the threat of extinction as endangered species. They love to visit remote primitive tribal cultures and make sure to take lots of photos of themselves with the indigenous inhabitants. Such primitive cultures are allowed to be as undiverse and unaccepting of the outside world as they want, because that simply adds to their charm.

The Muslim rejection of, and effort to prevent, assimilation into Western culture thus makes perfect sense to multiculturalists. Islam by its natural instincts seeks to rise to power, thus multiculturalism has served Islam well and continues to serve its Islamist agenda—unless the United States regains its sanity before it is too late.

I have a mental image of the goals of Islam in the West. Like Dracula, Islam seeks the submission of Western culture. It is slowly walking toward its new twenty-first-century victim; the victim is stepping toward Dracula in a hypnotic state and with a feeling of submission. It is tired of freedom and responsibility; it wants to embrace dependency on another. Where is the United States heading with its relationship with Islam? Will it end up like all of the great Middle Eastern civilizations that abandoned their innocence, growth, identities, languages, cultures, and values and submitted to the seduction of a clear-cut, black-or-white authoritarian state of submission? Will it accept a value system where the end justifies the means? Will the rebel bad-boy attraction of Islam win? I believe it is not too late and that we still have a chance to defeat all of these lures that Islam puts before us.

The multicultural trap that is strangling the United States and Western civilization must be invalidated to allow America to breathe. The impossible expectation that we can remain diverse and still live happily ever after needs to be extinguished. That expectation is unrealistic, cruel, and self-destructive. Multiculturalists refuse to acknowledge that the United States, superpower or not, undergoes the same dynamics for survival that all cultures must go through. It needs a cohesive cultural identity to survive. Yet America continues to be used and abused by idealists who have a superficial view of human nature and cultural development. America must never become the victim of an unnecessary experiment.

The United States must expose the devil it knows and the devil it does not know: the good twin and the bad twin of Islamic dualism. Muslims in the West are playing the game of good cop/bad cop with America. While one commits terrorist acts, the other says this has nothing to do with Islam. Yet the truth is that Islam is one and the same. The West must never buy into the propaganda of Islamist groups in the United States. It really does not matter who is hurting Western civilization, the good or the bad side of Islam—the violent jihadists or the stealth jihadists. Even Hitler must have had a good side, from someone's perspective. The devil we know and the devil we don't know are one and the same. America must never get entangled in Islam's orbit of no return.

Will Islam continue to survive and thrive, or will it come crashing down on the weight of its own sword? Chapter 8 will delve into this.

8

House of Cards:
The Downfall of
Islam as We Know It

Within the DNA of Islam is a self-destructive element: fear of the truth and a constant urge to fight those who value truth. Islam planted its own seed of destruction the day it relied on lies, violence, robbery, slavery, and rape for its expansion. For fourteen hundred years, Islamists have managed to suppress the truth about their religion to the majority of Muslims and have condoned acts of unspeakable injustices, violence, and torture by their prophet that must never be criticized under penalty of death. In the process, they have produced a morally confused and self-destructive culture that is incapable of withstanding challenges through honest debate or criticism. Challenging Islam with the truth brings out the worst in Muslim culture: shame, pride, envy, rage, lies, slander, violence, and terrorist acts. Muslims are educated to believe there is one solution for people who challenge Islam: "If you challenge my religion, I will kill you."

At its core, Islam is desperate for approval, and, as a consequence, it relies heavily on the outside world, seeking feedback that expresses respect, confirms its legitimacy, and even shows submission to Islam. If that is not received, all hell breaks loose with destructive acts not only toward the outside world, but also, strangely, against itself—Muslim against Muslim. Mohammed himself set the example for this dynamic when he not only destroyed those who rejected him, but also made enemies of Muslims who competed with him.

Toward the end of his life, in 631 C.E., Mohammed actually ordered the destruction and burning of a mosque that had been newly built by a Muslim tribe that lived a few miles north of Medina in an area called Quba. The builders of the mosque invited Mohammed to honor the new mosque with his presence: "O Messenger of God, we have built a mosque for the sick and needy and for rainy and cold nights, and we would like you to visit us and pray for us" (Tabari IX:61). Yet instead of going to bless the mosque, Mohammed commanded his fighters to "go to this mosque whose owners are unjust people and destroy and burn it" (Tabari IX:61). Mohammed's fighters destroyed the mosque while worshipers were still inside, and, as usual, Allah approved of this action in a verse in the Koran (9:107–110) that justified Mohammed's violence against other Muslims. After the destruction of the mosque, Mohammed told the people in the area that they could pray in the mosque he had built there. Mohammed called his mosque "more virtuous" than the one he had destroyed. Although the reason he gave for destroying the mosque was that its builders were unjust rivals, his actual motivation was pure envy, distrust, and a need to be the only person who performed acts of benefit for the community.

This was the example Mohammed set for what his followers should do if they did not like the actions of rivals—even if the rivals were Muslims. As a result, violence between Muslims reached epidemic proportions after Mohammed died. At least fifty thousand were killed in a single war over who would lead the caliphate. At that time, Aisha, Mohammed's widow, and her supporters, believed that Imam Ali was behind the murder of Othman, a companion of Mohammed and the third Caliph after Mohammed's death, and consequently fought Ali, Mohammed's only male blood relative, whose supporters believed he was the one entitled to head the caliphate. These wars and the resulting assassination of Ali were behind the Sunni and Shiite divide in Islam. Wars and assassinations became the destiny of the prophet's apostles (Sahaba), who fought and killed one another to determine the leadership of the growing Islamic empire. They followed Mohammed's advice when he said, "Whosoever of you *sees* an evil action, let him *change* it with his *hand.*" For several generations, every Muslim caliph was brutally killed by fellow Muslims over who should succeed the previous caliph.

The Islamic dream to return to the caliphate—which Muslims envision as the ultimate ideal of a peaceful and blissful Islamic political system—has no basis in reality. It never existed during Mohammed's time or any other time after his death. The caliphate had a bloody history of pitting Muslim against Muslim, sect against sect, and engaging in revolutions and counterrevolutions, all in the name of Islam. That was then, and it is still the same way today—the Islamic political system remains dysfunctional. Sunnis and Shiites blow up each other's mosques today in Iraq and other areas; Saudi Arabia discriminates against Shiites and burns their Korans. The Islamic caliphate was never a peaceful and just state.

Another factor that promoted rivalries, hatred, and violence among Muslim sects was a hadith by Mohammed. In it, he made a prediction that caused further divisions and accusations of apostasy between Muslims: "Seventy-two of the seventy-three Muslim sects will go to hell; only one of the sects will be in Paradise; it is the majority group" (Sunaan Abu Dawud, 3.40.4580). Mohammed never named that sect, but his prediction had devastating repercussions in Muslim relations, because each sect truly believed that the others would go to hell. Then and now, every sect of Islam accuses the others of apostasy, thus deserving to be killed. The result is an Islamic culture of no compromise and "I alone against the world."

Yet despite the hatred and animosity Muslim sects feel toward one another—and this is the paradox of Islam—all Muslims feel an obligation to present an image of unity, no matter how they feel toward one another. While instilling divisions and commandments to correct one another and reject the other's sins, Mohammed also commanded his followers to kill anyone who causes disunity: "Whoever creates disunity in the Islamic community, kill him" (Sunaan Abu Dawud, 3.40.4744). Mohammed did not clearly define disunity and left it in the hands of Muslims to be judge, jury, and executioner of those whom they believe are causing disunity among them. Thus, many Muslims today feel justified in interpreting calls for Western-style democracy in the Muslim world as causing disunity among Muslims. Because there is no central authority in Islam to decide matters of who is causing disunity and who is not, the commandment to kill Muslims who cause disunity can be interpreted by any sect as justification to act against the other. The bottom line is that this lack of clarity and conflict in what Mohammed commanded has caused a mess inside Muslim society, especially in its political system, leading to lawlessness and turmoil up until the present. Demonstrations, violence, and deaths continued to take place in Tahrir Square for months after the revolution.

Islam's internal conflict emanates from Mohammed's own personal struggle at its inception. Islamic literature has documented in great detail how Mohammed suffered from bodily spasms, twitching, visions, uncontrollable lip movements, severe abdominal pains, sweating, fear, and anxiety, all of which led him to have suicidal thoughts. Mohammed's foster mother, Halima, brought him back to his biological mother and told her that he was possessed. When Mohammed was an adult, he suffered doubts about his own sanity, but his first wife, Khadija, told him that these were signs of his prophethood.[1]

This description of what Mohammed suffered from in his early life and adulthood was taught in Islamic studies classes that I took in school, but the way his symptoms were explained to us was different from how a psychiatrist would diagnose them today. What we learned was similar to what Mohammed's wife told him: that he was communicating with the angel Gabriel, who brought him the words of the Koran from Allah. Muslims all around the world today still believe this to be the truth behind Mohammed's symptoms, fears, and anxiety.

Incredibly, Mohammed himself was not at peace with his own message. He was not optimistic about the future of Islam and Muslims: "the Messenger of Allah [Mohammed] observed: Verily Islam started as something strange and it would again revert [to its old position] of being strange just as it started, and it would recede between the two mosques just as the serpent crawls back into its hole" (Sahih Muslim B1 N0270).

In this hadith, Mohammed foretold that the end of Islam would be strange, just as its beginning had been, because it would shrink back to the limited area it had come from— between the two mosques of Mecca and Medina. Could that prediction by Muhammad be a sign of the inevitable demise of Islam? Will Muslims ever understand that Islam and sharia should not be a part of government? Will the Tahrir Square revolutionaries and their counterparts in other Middle Eastern countries finally learn that their enemies are not the Mubaraks, the Assads, or the Gaddafis, but the seventh-century political system that still rules them today? Will Muslims from Morocco to Indonesia reject sharia and send it back to where it came from, to the two mosques in Mecca and Medina? Only time will tell.

Mohammed's predictions of Islam crawling back like a snake to where it came from were repeated extensively in several other of his hadiths:

> "Belief returns and goes back to Medina like a snake." (Sahih Bukhari V3B30 N100)

> "Muslims will be the scum and the rubbish even though their numbers may increase; the enemy will

not fear Muslims anymore. This will be because the Muslims will love world and dislike death." (Sunaan Abu Dawud, 37.4284)

"Muhammad's contemporaries were the best Muslims; after three generations, the Muslims will be mainly treacherous and untrustworthy." (Sahih Bukhari V5B57N2, 3)

"There will be much killing during the last days of the Muslim."(Bukhari V9B88N183)

"Verily, Belief returns and goes back to Medina as a snake returns and goes back to its hole [when in danger]." (Bukhari V3B30N100)

Mohammed also predicted a large movement of apostates out of Islam:

"Muslims will diminish in number and they will go back to where they started [before Islam]." (Sunaan Abu Dawud, 2.19.3029)

"There will be no trace of Islam in some believers." (Bukhari V9B84N65)

"There will appear in this nation . . . a group of people so pious apparently that you will consider your prayers inferior to their prayers, but they will recite the Quran, the teachings of which will not go beyond their throats and will go out of their religion as an arrow darts through the game, whereupon the archer may look at his arrow, its Nasl at its Risaf and its Fuqa to see whether it is blood-stained or not [that is, they will have not even a trace of Islam in them]." (Bukhari V9B84N65)

Mohammed was so consumed with the survival and legitimacy of Islam that he expressed extreme feelings of fear that Muslims would abandon Islam. Such fears caused him to severely punish anyone who rejected or abandoned him, which drove him into a life of never-ending battle and mass murder. As a result, he did not present a coherent ideology that could produce a stable and peaceful society. Although he demanded unity from Muslims, his actions did not support unity, especially when he destroyed the mosque of his rivals. Even while telling Muslims that Islam would survive to rule the world under a caliphate, he also said that Islam would end after three generations and would eventually crawl back to where it came from. No functioning system can be based on such confusion and conflicting messages, which are rife in the Koran, the Hadith, and, as I have described, the example of Mohammed himself.

Why, then, after Mohammed died, did Arabs hold onto Islam and strive to preserve it through horrific bloodshed? Why did various tribes compete for leadership and kill one another, especially those who abandoned Islam? The answer is simple: Islam gave enormous wealth and power to Mohammed's successors, the caliphs, who followed in his footsteps. Since its inception, Islam has been at war with civilization, bringing down one culture after another. Such civilizations were considered a threat to Arabia's identity and culture, and with Islam, it was the outside world that had to change and adapt to Arabia's language, culture, and religion. Islam became the perfect formula for totalitarian control and submission, which served the Arabian Peninsula well. Arab tribes no longer had to battle one another over scarce desert resources. Arabs no longer needed to travel far to trade in order to survive, because people throughout the Middle East flocked to Mecca to perform the Haj, bringing in wealth from all over the world. Under Islam, the extreme ethnocentric culture of Arabia became immune to the impact of alien religions and cultures when non-Muslims were forbidden from touching the holy grounds of Mecca and Medina. Keeping non-Muslims out is still a priority of Saudi Arabia. When united under Islam, once desert-poor Arabia was set forever.

As a result, Muslim rulers had to preserve the goose that laid the golden eggs: Islam. Yet they soon realized that they could not rely merely on the Koran, with its many contradictions, to rule the new conquered lands, which were not familiar with Arabian culture. To rule effectively, 150 years after Mohammed died, they created a holy decree, sacred laws called sharia. These laws were based on the Koran, Mohammed's lifestyle, and the Hadith, sayings that were still being gathered during that time by several Islamic authorities and sects, who provided both similar and different hadiths. Whenever the caliph needed a specific law, somehow a hadith was found to support it. Some Muslims claim that several hadiths were not correct or *Sahih*, but they remain in Islamic books because certain laws of sharia were based on them.

Islam's attraction was infectious. Some of the conquered nations found the Islamic legal system beneficial because its laws made it easier for tyrannies to survive if their legitimacy seemed to come from Allah's law itself. Consequently, for fourteen hundred years, both Muslims and non-Muslims in the Middle East have been governed by the most brutal religious, political, and legal system the world has ever seen. Today, the ultimate success or failure of Middle Eastern revolutions relies on accepting or rejecting sharia as the state legal system. So far, not one Muslim country has declared after its revolution that sharia will not be the state law. This means that Middle Eastern revolutions are sadly going to fail once again. Until today, no Muslim country has dared to reject the stranglehold of sharia, especially with Saudi petro-dollars in the equation.

From its inception, Islam could not survive without state enforcement. Islam became the state, and the state became Islam. It is the only system that Muslims and their leaders have ever known and lived under, century after century. The pain of sharia's tyranny was—and still is—regarded as an indisputable part of the life that God himself wants Muslims to live by. When the pressure of tyranny becomes intolerable and expresses itself in violent reprisals against the Islamic state, it has to be redirected toward the outside world. This is how Islam has survived for many centuries. As long as this formula worked with little interruption, things were tolerable.

When Islamic terrorism against the outside world was met with an international outcry, especially after 9/11, Muslim governments were forced to do the dangerous job of cracking down on the terrorists who ran amok all over the Muslim world. Much of this crackdown was superficial and only for show, but the terrorist activity did subside for a while, causing the pressure to build up internally.

Internal uprising, violence, and terrorism against Muslim governments became inevitable. Now that the enemy outside of Islam is fighting back, the violence, as it always has, has returned to where it originated—within the tormented Muslim society. Yet this time it has been given a pretty name: the Arab Spring. In reality, though, it is another aspect of the never-ending self-destructive Islamic cycle. If it does not express itself externally, then it will explode internally.

In a culture where the word *peace* has little value and violent jihad is everything, sooner or later the internal pressure must be dealt with. Soon after the January revolution, the interim Egyptian government, which had close ties with Islamist groups, started a new round of fearmongering propaganda, in an attempt to redirect the anger on the street back toward the outside world. As an example, in June 2011, a young American student at Emory University School of Law, Ilan Grapel, was arrested by the Egyptian authorities on charges of being a "highly trained" spy for Israel. The headlines, printed in red in all major Egyptian newspapers, including *Al Ahram*, stated, "An Israeli Officer Participated in the Revolution to Insert Division and Distrust between the People and the Military." Other headlines claimed, "The Spy Participated in the Fitna between Muslims and Christians in Maspiro [a suburb in Cairo]." Such fabricated arrests of Westerners are a terrible game that Muslim governments often resort to when things get out of control. To the savvy Egyptian, such games are laughable fabrications, but unfortunately these tactics do work on the psyches of most Egyptians, who are told that the Israeli Mossad was part of the conspiracy against the Egyptian military in Tahrir Square.

The Egyptian government, the media, and Islamists have played such games too many times to distract and frighten Egyptians into unity. Ilan, who was born in the United States, does have dual Israeli citizenship, but that is hardly evidence that he is a spy. Despite his mother's pleas that such charges are totally fabricated against her son, who traveled to Egypt to volunteer for a nonprofit organization that helped African refugees in Egypt, the U.S. media have shown little interest in his ordeal.

Whether before or after the revolution, Egyptian leaders resorted to the same old cycle of lies and violence, acts that are allowed under sharia. As a teenager during the 1967 war, I remember similar lies about the war and accusations of espionage against the few Egyptian Jews who were left in Egypt. One of them, a fellow student from 1967 to almost 1970 at the American University in Cairo, saw her male family members dragged to jail for three years. Those poor Egyptian Jews were put in Egyptian jails for nothing and suffered unspeakable torture and humiliation until they were expelled from Egypt. I met some of them in the United States many years later and asked them about their memories of the mistreatment. To my surprise, they have shown true grace and decency and have chosen to talk about the good memories they have of Egypt. I am honored to have some of them as my friends today.

Muslim governments have felt a need to lie at the highest levels, in order to bring Muslims closer together. Lying for the best interest of the Islamic state has become a semi-holy act that a good Muslim feels obliged to do, when in reality it has become an Islamic mental disease that must be exposed for what it is: spreading falsehoods against non-Muslims for the benefit of Islamic unity. Islamists' dysfunctional tactic of using any means to achieve their goals is out of control. The Islamic tools of the trade for problem solving are lies, hate propaganda, fearmongering, distortions, exaggerations, and slander, used in conjunction with threats, violence, and terrorist acts—all of which are allowed under the laws of Islam. Muslim sheikhs have never abandoned this Islamic legacy, which goes back to Mohammed, and it has become the default method of problem solving. It is the solution before Islamic revolutions and after Islamic revolutions; not much change in areas that desperately need change.

The truth is fiercely challenged and denied and is met with lies and fabrications. The day this dysfunctional cycle ends will be a day of true freedom that will liberate the Muslim people. The majority of them are poor victims who are unaware of the real problem. What the Muslim people really needed to accomplish when they revolted on January 2011, but they could not verbalize it, was to end the curse of lying that has infected Muslim society from top to bottom, especially Islamic clerics who have forgotten the value of truth telling. Success can only come to a society based on truth.

The question, then, is how can a religion that perpetuates lies and violence for the sake of its God end such a destructive cycle? We all know the quote often attributed to Abraham Lincoln: "You may fool all the people some of the time, you can even fool some of the people all of the time, but you cannot fool all of the people all the time." Islam is probably the best example for this popular saying. Islam has managed to fool "some of the people" all of the time for more than fourteen hundred years because this deceptive characteristic of Islam is rooted so deeply that most Muslims keep falling for it, over and over. When Muslims immigrate to the United States, they often say of Americans, "They are so honest!" Muslims envy Americans for this, yet they live in denial of the fact that the Koran commands them to lie to promote Islam.

What is Islam afraid of? Of its documented bloody history? Of feeling deep shame because its prophet slaughtered both Arabs and Jews? Of the slaughter that continued afterward and up to this day? Of the lies and the cover-up? The answer is all of the above, plus even more hidden scandals yet to come that will strike at the heart and soul of Islam.

A major challenge to Islam has been building up. Muslims have always expressed their pride and superiority by claiming that their holy book, the Koran, has never been corrupted and that its words came directly from Allah, while criticizing the Bible for having been corrupted, reworded, and changed, without people having any proof of what the original words were. For centuries, Muslims have worn this as their badge of honor, even when non-Muslims didn't criticize their Koran.

Yet this badge of honor will soon be questioned by the 1972 discovery of the oldest Koran in Sanaa, Yemen. While making repairs to a very old mosque, workers found a huge number of Islamic manuscripts, and the Yemeni government sought the help of German scholars in uncovering the mystery of their origin. What the Germans discovered was that the present Koran was different from these early manuscripts, casting doubt on Islam's long-held claims about the Koran. The Yemeni government, interestingly, instead of welcoming the discovery, started a process of cover-up and quickly withdrew the project, ending the research in 1985.

Microfilms and copies of documents are available, even though not yet released to the public. Will the Germans soon write a book about their discovery? Or will they fear the Islamic fatwa of death that will certainly follow anyone who exposes the weak points in Islam? Incidentally, there is a law in sharia that states that non-Muslims who expose the weaknesses of Islam have committed a serious crime "called enormity," which could carry the death penalty. This is another layer to the Islamic fear of the truth. The discovery disproves Islamic claims that the Koran is infallible and that it is Allah's original revelation, word for word. Will this shocking discovery cause the downfall of Islam that Mohammed predicted? Only time will tell.[2]

My prediction is that Muslims will accuse the Germans of falsifying the documents and will call non-Muslim Germans Islamophobes and racists. The world will see yet another enormous Islamic cover-up of the Sanaa Koran, proving that Muslims, not only Mohammed, are active participants in, and promoters of, a certain reality about Islam. Islam has met a deep need in the psyche of many cultures in the Middle East that has made Muslims eager to protect and preserve it. Right after Mohammed's death, that process was initiated by the caliph Uthman, when he standardized the Koran and produced one copy and burned all of the others.

Islam is probably the only religion on earth today that hates any new discovery about its origin. Only God knows what secrets have been hidden, omitted, or inserted by Arabs to make Islam a perfect fit for their needs. The enormous number of contradictions in the Koran does not reflect well on Allah, who is supposed to be the author. In order to resolve its contradictions, Muslims and Allah himself in the

Koran suggested the concept of abrogation, which means that if there is a contradiction, the earlier verses should be abrogated. Yet how could Allah decide that what he said earlier was wrong and must be changed?

The Sanaa discovery is not known to the majority of Muslims. Most of the Muslims I communicate with have no idea about that important find in Yemen. You would think that Muslims would be happy to uncover the ancient manuscript, debating it and discussing it everywhere in the halls of their educational institutions, but it is just the opposite. No one is eager to teach Muslims about it. That can only prove one thing: Muslim leaders are actively participating in a cover-up for fear of mass apostasy, because the discovery makes the present Koran illegitimate.

This is just one of the many secrets, lies, and cover-ups behind Islam's raging anger and worldwide terrorism, secrets that must be protected by any means. Since its inception, Islam has been extremely vulnerable and has built a formidable image on shaky grounds. Islam's decay is partly caused by the acts of those who are protecting its image from the truth. The Sanaa Koran could end up being the last straw that will push Islam to crumble like a house of cards.

Muslim countries will not experience internal or external peace as long as their top priority is to cover up the truth from an increasingly angry, poor, and desperate Muslim population, while using violence against anyone who dares uncover such a truth. The cycle of lies, cover-up, and violence must be exposed and stopped.

The reason Muslims cannot forgive and forget their disputes with the outside world is because they espouse a religion that does not allow self-forgiveness. That is why

Muslim borders with non-Muslim countries are excessively bloody and hostile. Poverty-stricken Muslim countries have developed extreme envy of the prosperity of their non-Muslim neighbors. That is how Mohammed felt toward his Jewish neighbor tribes. Today Islamic leaders are seeing a good portion of their population running away toward enemy land, non-Muslim land, instead of joining the fight. Muslims are pouring into Europe and the United States for work, as well as into India from Bangladesh and Pakistan, again for a better life in countries that Islamic jihadists aim to conquer and terrorize to turn Islamic. For Muslim leadership, the cycle of envy and Islamic immigration due to dissatisfaction with life in the Muslim state has become an opportunity to spread both violent and stealthy jihad in the new countries that Muslims migrate to. The last thing on the minds of Islamic leaders is to learn from others and reform themselves; instead, they send jihadists and Islamists to follow Muslim immigrants into their new homes.

The jihadist plan is to keep Muslim immigrants in line and prevent them from assimilating. Of course, not all Muslim immigrants fall into this trap, but, unfortunately, many do. The jihadist plan is to keep pushing the envelope to test how far Western countries will go to bend to the demands of Muslims. The ultimate plan is to suck out the blood of Western civilization—its success and glory—and claim it later for Islam. That is what Islamists did long ago to the great Egyptian and Persian civilizations, until they were no longer great. Then Islamists moved farther east and west to other great civilizations in Spain and the Far East to do the same. A respected Egyptian journalist, Ata Abd Al-Aal, recently said, "The

U.S. will be transformed into an Islamic republic; the most important place for the future of islam, after Mecca and Medina, is the U.S."[3] The plan is to make the United States another holy land, probably on the hallowed earth of Ground Zero.

Islam has developed a relentless need to expand into non-Muslim lands to end its citizens' pain of envy and as an outlet for the poverty and despair that are by-products of life in the Islamic state. The last hope for Islam today is expansion into the West, and the steps for achieving this are detailed in the manuals of the Muslim Brotherhood. The following excerpts are quoted from the Muslim Brotherhood's "phased plan" for accomplishing its mission:

> Phase One: Discreet and secret establishment of leadership.
> Phase Two: Gradual appearance on the public scene, exercising and utilizing various public activities. [This has already been done.]
> Phase Three: Escalation, prior to conflict and confrontation with the rulers, through utilizing mass media. [This is currently in progress.]
> Phase Four: Open public confrontation with the government through exercising the political pressure approach. [This is being aggressively pursued today.] Training on the use of weapons domestically and overseas in anticipation of zero-hour. [It has noticeable activities in this regard.]
> Phase Five: Seizing power to establish the Islamic Nation under which all parties and Islamic groups are united.[4]

The previous scheme has been tested and has proved successful over and over against many great nations, much more sophisticated than the Arabian Peninsula was when it was conquered. A much later example was the 1947 partition of India when Pakistan was carved out of India and made into an Islamic state. More recent examples are Kosovo and Chechnya; the latter is still demanding secession from Russia. Islamic power is measured by how many countries Muslims have conquered and controlled. Like Dracula, Islam needs to suck new blood in order to survive. This is also how the Islamic Dracula circles its prey, right on U.S. campuses. A video posted on the Internet caught an Islamic chaplain at Vanderbilt University promoting bizarre ideas to predominantly Muslim American students.[5] The chaplain, Awad Binhazim, said the following:

1. Muslims should work to institute sharia law in the United States.
2. Muslims should not become Westernized and must confront the West.
3. The Torah and the Bible have been falsified by corrupt rabbis and priests.
4. Islam doesn't allow for personal choice.
5. Islam demands that homosexuals be put to death.
6. Muslims discovered America before Columbus did.

Note that number six is a serious claim by many Muslims who, in their minds, want to justify jihad to their students and to jihadists—to encourage them to feel victimized by the American culture that was taken away from Muslims, who are the original discoverers of America. The same dynamic is at play regarding Jerusalem, which Muslims claim is a Muslim holy land and that Jews came and took it from Muslims. This kind of education is now being accepted on U.S. campuses as a religious right. The infiltration has succeeded, and Islam is now sucking the new blood that will keep it alive for a few more centuries. Western democracies are now feeding the needs of Islam and engaging it, which can only result in extending the lifeline it desperately needs. Without the extension in its lifeline that the West is providing to Islam, it is doomed to die exactly the way that Mohammed himself predicted.

If new blood is not available, Islam will turn inward against itself. Islam cannot live with itself for long, because whenever the temperature of human pain and suffering rises, the political system gets infected with revolutions, counter-revolutions, and assassinations, which is what is happening internally to Islamic states now.

Again, the success of Islam is measured by how many countries it controls—not by how many hearts it has touched and blessed. Islamic society rejects citizens who want freedom and democracy, and it covers up its true intentions toward protesters and revolutionaries by lying to numb the brains of its own Muslim citizens, to keep them from thinking for themselves, and to keep them occupied as the foot soldiers they must be for the purpose of holy jihad. Engaging in truly democratic and peaceful diplomacy with the rest of the world will not bring Muslims the glory that Islam has convinced them they deserve. Muslims who are moving the wheels of jihad realize that if they engage the world in a policy of live and let live, they will lose their power and will implode.

Like a Ponzi scheme, Islam must expand to survive. The Ponzi scheme works as long as it keeps expanding. In that sense, Islam works only when more and more people join the pyramid of Islam. As long as the supply of new Muslim believers can empower the pyramid, it will convince the other suckers, the naive Muslim followers, that they are right. Muslims are always eager to report on the masses in the West who are converting to Islam because they believe that it will encourage Muslims to stay in the religion. Yet when the light of truth reaches the pyramid, especially the majority on the bottom, who are not benefiting from the system and who are being sacrificed to preserve and perpetuate the fraud, then the whole system will collapse, and the colossal deception will be exposed.

Totalitarian, political, legal, and jihadist Islam has defied all odds with its extraordinary revival in the twenty-first century. It has received an enormous degree of tolerance and respect from Western democracies. Yet could that revival be Islam's last gasp that will end its fourteen-hundred-year tyranny? Or will the West provide Islam with its much-needed blood transfusion, in the form of acceptance and inclusion, which will further prolong the life of the Islamic Dracula? That is the challenge Western democracies must eventually face. The right choice will be to reject Islam as it is practiced today, to contain it and discredit it. For that to happen, the West must undo many of its policies toward Islam and Muslim countries.

Conclusion

The epidemic of Islamic terrorism, civil unrest, wars, and revolutions is nothing but a symptom of panic over Islam's downfall. It is a desperate cry for help, for new blood to rescue it. If it were not for petro-dollars, Islam would have died a natural death after World War II, together with the Nazi ideology. Petro-dollars have come to the rescue and sustained it. Yet despite their wealth from oil, Muslim countries have again reached an alarming level of stagnation, poverty, and demoralization, similar to that of seventh-century Arabia, when Islam burst out of the Arabian Peninsula searching for new blood. The Arab street will never admit to a Westerner how desperate Muslims are, but many former Muslims, I among them, can sense the desperation. The situation is truly scary, because Arab media and Islamic leaders are directing all of the rage seen in Arab capitals toward the evil great Satan and the little Satan, the United States and Israel.

Muslim jihadists have their plans set on the greatest prize of all—to conquer the United States—and they won't give up easily. As I have described, it is their lifeline. The

West is a great land for expansion that could revive a dying religion. Without this rich lifeline from America, Muslim nations will continue to be plagued with revolutions and bloody civil wars, until ultimately they self-destruct, together with as many other civilizations as they can take down with them. That will be an Armageddon.

Western civilization has no idea that it is entrusted with the enormous responsibility of saving humanity. This is much more important than saving endangered species and more essential than stopping climate change, because if Islam wins, all such Western efforts will cease, because they are not Islamic values. The West must never be tolerant of an intolerant ideology that seeks to destroy it. Western countries must trust and use their basic "survival instincts" to neutralize an enemy made up of jihadist killer robots. The West can go down in history as the civilization that saved the world and gave our children a brighter future, or it can be remembered for having revived and prolonged the life of the most morbidly dysfunctional ideology that humanity has seen.

Islam will collapse like a house of cards and crumble under its own weight if the West does not provide it with a life line. Once the Western "infidels" learn about the secret life of Islam, it is simply a matter of watching Islam implode, liberating more than a billion people. Islam is the biggest lie in human history and cannot survive a confrontation with the truth. Nevertheless, it is a lie that 1.2 billion souls have fallen for. Yet Islam has sown the seeds of its own collapse, because it must repeatedly suppress the truth and promote lies and propaganda against individuals and cultures that promote the truth. The more that Western ideas penetrate into Muslim society, the harder and faster Islam's propaganda must come. How long can Islamists sustain such lies and illusions in this day and age? It all depends on how hard we make it for them.

The ideology of Islam has had too many victims, mostly Muslims themselves. The primary beneficiaries of the fall of political and legal Islam will be Muslims themselves. Tyrannical Islam will collapse when the civilized world exposes it for what it is and rejects it; when its leaders get tired of their lies, fabrications, and incitement against innocent victims; and when Islamists are discredited and disrespected and no longer given funds to enable terror groups and jihadist individuals.

Islam dictates that victims at the bottom of the Muslim heap must never be allowed to communicate or have access to free inquiry. Islamic borders must shun, repel, and defeat any exposure to the truth. Islam's borders with non-Muslim countries pose a threat to its need to withhold exposure to the truth. No religion or ideology can survive if the truth is not on its side. Islam has succeeded in surviving for fourteen hundred years by repeatedly hiding from the truth. It has become a dinosaur that cannot survive in today's environment; it has no solutions to modern problems and will eventually go extinct. Yet as it moves toward its demise, will it bring the world down with it or will it go quietly? This depends on the courage of free societies.

If the United States and Europe continue to embrace Islam, bloody wars will be inevitable, both externally against Muslim nations and, worse still, internally in the United States, in the form of a civil war after Muslims strengthen their grip on the U.S. political system. Tahrir Square can happen in the United States fifty years from now. A Chechnya-like scenario, with a country controlled by a separatist movement, can occur in Western Europe in ten or twenty years. If nothing is done, we can merely delay it. Sooner or later, there will be a deadly war if we fail to do something now.

I dreamed and still dream of a real Arab Spring, where the majority of the people will stand behind an enlightened leader at Tahrir Square in a magical moment of truthful courage and say, "We need to change course and to change ourselves. What we suffer from is not imposed on us by Mubarak, but by Islam controlling the state and the legal system, and this must end. It is time for the snake of sharia to retreat back to Mecca, so that we can liberate beautiful Egypt, Persia, and the rest of the Middle East from this Arabian cultural curse." If Muslim nations reject such an enlightened leader and continue to seek an Islamic Ummah, then the future of stability and peace in the Islamic world will be grim indeed.

The world is eagerly waiting to embrace a new and better relationship with the Muslim world. Unlike conventional Arab wisdom, it is in the West's strategic best interests to cultivate the stability it seeks in the Middle East through the development of free and democratic political systems. No Western nation wishes to see or support Islamic dictatorships that oppress their people, because that dynamic sooner or later blows up in everyone's face. The West has treated Muslim countries with kid gloves and has shown extreme self-restraint, understanding, and patience, in light of the last three or four decades of worldwide Islamic terrorism and jihad. Western countries are ready to admit their mistakes and take responsibility for their actions, to forgive and forget and even accept the Islamic excuses, instead of apologies. Yet is the Muslim world ready to do the same?

The Muslim masses are yearning for truth and respect for their dignity, humanity, and rights. They deserve all of this. Arab children are the face of the future, and they, above all, deserve it. When will Muslim leaders realize that they must back away from the game and peacefully allow Islam to be only a religion, a relationship between man and God that should never have become God's punishment on earth?

Notes

2. Why Islamic Revolutions Are Doomed to Fail

1. Al Kamra TV, May 8, 2011, www.youtube.com/watch?v=LRO_
   rT_bRU0&feature=share, translated by Nonie Darwish; minor
   changes in the order of some words to make it comprehensible.
2. "Director of National Intelligence James Clapper: Muslim
   Brotherhood 'Largely Secular'," February 10, 2011, http://
   abcnews.go.com/blogs/politics/2011/02/director-of-national-
   inteligence-james-clapper-muslim-brotherhood-largely-secular/.
3. *Reliance of the Traveler*, al-Misri, o25.5, p. 644.
4. Ibid., o9.9, p. 603.
5. Ibid., o9.0, p. 599.
6. Ibid., o25.3, p. 640.
7. Ibid., o25.5, p. 644.
8. Imam Abu Hanifa, *Codified Islamic Law*, vol. 3, 914C.
9. Walter Isaacson, *Benjamin Franklin: An American Life*, (New
   York: Simon and Schuster, 2003), p. 56.

3. A Muslim's Burden: How Islam Fails the Individual

1. "Egyptian Shaykh: Jihad Is Solution to Muslims' Financial
   Problems," May 31, 2011, http://translating-jihad.blogspot
   .com/2011/05/egyptian-shaykh-jihad-is-solution-to.html.

2. See http://www.youm7.com/News.asp?NewsID=418971& and Raymond Ibrahim, "Raped and Ransacked in the Muslim World," http://www.meforum.org/2920/raped-and-ransacked-in-the-muslim-world.

3. "American Peace Commissioners to John Jay,: March 28, 1786, Thomas Jefferson Papers, Series 1, General Correspondence, 1651–1827, Library of Congress, March 28, 1786.

4. *Reliance of the Traveler*, al-Misri, R10.3, p. 784.

5. Ibid., R8.2, p. 745.

6. Ibid., R2.16, p. 737.

7. Ibid., o9.0, p. 599.

8. Ibid., o16.5, p. 617.

9. Hava Lazarus-Yafeh, *Some Religious Aspects of Islam: A Collection of Articles*, (Leiden: Brill, 1981), p. 48.

10. Syed Abul 'Ala Maudoodi, *Towards Understanding Islam*, trans. and ed. By Khurshid Ahmad (Falls Church, VA: World Assembly of Mulsim Youth, 1980), 78.

11. *Reliance of the Traveler*, al-Misri, w29.3, p. 915.

12. Ibid., o25.3, p. 640.

4. Israel amid Islamic Tornadoes

1. Pew Research Center, New Global Attitudes Project, http://www.pewglobal.org/2011/04/25/egyptians-embrace-revolt-leaders-religious-parties-and-military-as-well/1/r.

2. "Why Jimmy the Dhimmi Hates Israel?" May 30, 2008, http://israelmatzav.blogspot.com/2008/05/why-jimmy-dhimmi-hates-israel.html.

3. "Muslim Brotherhood's Egyptian Leader Mohammed Badie: 'Waging Jihad Is Mandatory,'" www.freerepublic.com/focus/news/2666863/posts.

4. "After Fall of Mubarak, Group Announces Intent to Form Nazi Party," www.almasryalyoum.com/en/node/451086.

5. See http://www.alarabiya.net/articles/2011/06/07/152291.html.

6. "Muslims Believe U.S. Seeks to Undermine Islam," April 24, 2007, http://www.worldpublicopinion.org/pipa/articles/brmideastnafricara/346.php.

7. Qatar TV, January 9, 2009.

8. Al-Rahma TV, January 17, 2009.
9. Abdul Malik bin Hisham, ed., *Authoritative Islamic History: The Life of Mohammad "Sirat Rasul Allah" by Muhammad bin Ishaq (d. 773 AD)*, trans. Alfred Guillaume; *The Life of Muhammad*, p. 461; see also Tabari VIII, p. 27.
10. Bin Hisham, *Authoritative Islamic History*, p. 461.
11. Ibid., p. 464.
12. Ibid.
13. Sirat, p. 463; Tabari VIII, p. 33.
14. Tabari VIII, p. 116; Ishaq, p. 511.

5. Exodus: The Rise of Islamic Apostasy

1. "Translating Jihad," http://translating-jihad.blogspot.com.
2. "Source of the Punishment for Apostasy," www.onislam.net/english/ask-the-scholar/crimes-and-penalties/apostasy/169569.html.
3. Ibid.
4. Translation of fatwa, http://en.wikipedia.org/wiki/File:Rechtsgutachten_betr_Apostasie_im_Islam.jpg.
5. Ali Sina, "Islam in Fast Demise," http://faithfreedom.org/oped/sina31103.htm.
6. "Magdi Allam Recounts His Path to Conversion," letter to the editor, *Corriere della Sera*, March 23, 2008.

6. Will the Arab Spring Usher In a Feminist Movement?

1. "Kuwaiti Politicians Debate Why Women Were Not Elected to Parliament," http://www.memritv.org/clip/en/1633.htm.
2. Interview aired on Al-Hurra TV, January 13, 2008, http://www.memritv.org/clip_transcript/en/1657.htm.
3. Leila Ahmed, "Veil of Ignorance," http://www.foreignpolicy.com/articles/2011/04/25/veil_of_ignorance?page=0,0.
4. See Jihad Watch, http://www.jihadwatch.org/archives/018595.php.

7. Western Vulnerability

1. "Kuwaiti Prof Suggests a Biological Attack on White House, Prays for Bombing of Nuclear Plant on Lake

Michigan," http://www.memrijttm.org/content/en/report
.htm?report=3085&param=APT.
2. "The American Psyche, Post-9/11," http://www.webmd.com/
balance/features/american-psyche-post-911.
3. Ibid.
4. "Terror in America (26) Muslim Leaders: A Wave of Conversion
to Islam in the U.S. following September 11," November 18,
2001, http://www.memri.org/report/en/0/0/0/0/0/0/550.htm.
5. Thomas Kaplan, "At State Senate Meeting on Threats to City,
a Tense Debate over Islamic Terror," *New York Times*, April 8,
2011, http://www.nytimes.com/2011/04/09/nyregion/09hearing
.html?_r=1.
6. "U.S. Muslims Honor Imam Khomeini Legacy," June 4, 2011,
http://www.presstv.ir/detail/183152.html.
7. "Remarks by the President on a New Beginning,"
June 4, 2009, http://www.whitehouse.gov/the-press-office/
remarks-president-cairo-university-6-04-09.
8. Ibid.
9. Walid Shoebat and Ben Barrack, "Weiner's In-laws and the
Secret Muslim Brotherhood Connections Revealed," http://
www.shoebat.com/documents/secretConnections.htm.
10. "U.S. Government Support for Gulen," http://www.meforum
.org/2045/fethullah-gulens-grand-ambition#_ftnref49.
11. Erick Stakelbeck, "The Gulen Movement: A New Islamic
World Order?" June 4, 2011, http://www.cbn.com/cbnnews/
world/2011/May/The-Gulen-Movement-The-New-Islamic-
World-Order/.

8. House of Cards: The Downfall of Islam as We Know It

1. *The Life of Muhammad*, pp. 71–72, 106–155.
2. "Would the Earliest Quranic Manuscripts of Sana's Spell the
Downfall of Islam?" June 28, 2009, http://www.islam-watch
.org/index.php?option=com_content&task=view&id=46&Ite
mid=58.
3. See http://www.memritv.org/clip/en/0/0/0/0/0/0/2735.htm.

4. Undated Muslim Brotherhood paper titled "Phases of the World Underground Movement Plan," http://bigpeace .com/fgaffney/2011/07/02/the-tipping-point-embracing-the-muslim-brotherhood/.

5. Bob Unruh, "Muslim Student Advisor, 'Death Penalty for "Gays,"' " *World Net Daily*, January 29, 2010, http://www.wnd .com/?pageId=123450; Grace Aviles, "Vanderbilt 'Muslims in the Military' Event Goes Viral," January 28, 2010, http://www .insidevandy.com/drupal/node/12594.

Index

Page numbers in *italics* refer to illustrations.